The Fosse Style

By Debra McWaters

Foreword by Ben Vereen

Prologue by Mindy Aloff

Copyright 2008 by Debra McWaters
Prologue copyright 2008 by Mindy Aloff
Printed in the United States of America on acid-free paper
All rights reserved
Photos of the Fosse dancers were taken by D. Thomas Porter, Ph.D.
The photos of Ben Vereen and Debra McWaters are by Don Jones.

13 12 11 10 09 08   6 5 4 3 2 1

Library of Congress Cataloging-in-Publication Data
McWaters, Debra.
The Fosse style / by Debra McWaters; foreword by Ben Vereen; prologue by Mindy Aloff.
p. cm.
ISBN 978-0-8130-3154-5 (cloth : alk. paper)—ISBN 978-0-8130-3153-8 (pbk. : alk. paper)
1. Jazz dance—Study and teaching. 2. Fosse, Bob, 1927-1987. I. Title.
GV1784.M38 2008
793.3—dc22   2007027540

The University Press of Florida is the scholarly publishing agency for the State University
System of Florida, comprising Florida A&M University, Florida Atlantic University, Florida
Gulf Coast University, Florida International University, Florida State University, New College
of Florida, University of Central Florida, University of Florida, University of North Florida,
University of South Florida, and University of West Florida.

University Press of Florida
15 Northwest 15th Street
Gainesville, FL 32611-2079
www.upf.com

For my mother and father

Contents

Ben Vereen

Foreword

To have worked with Bob Fosse is to have had your hand directly on the pulse of life. On the outside the work may look wonderfully stylish and easy; however, it comes from that inner pulse of life. "Demanding," "strenuous," and a "task master" are the criticisms most dancers make. But as Bob would say, "If you learn to dance this way, you'll dance for the rest of your life." I know my experiences and work with Bob have kept me dancing, learning, and living with my hand on the pulse.

This book is an example and expression of the intricate moves of the Fosse technique. Debra McWaters has taken on the task of writing this book and I must say has executed it very well by bringing to you a step-by-step look into the movement of Fosse. She is giving you the visual characteristics that made Fosse a signature style that is recognized worldwide.

Deb McWaters teaches you more than just the trademarks of his work, which you must internalize in order to understand and create. Fosse always worked his dancers. He would have us rehearse the same step over and over again until it was perfected, then go to lunch, come back, and work some more on the same step until it was absolutely pristine. For Fosse dancers and those who applied themselves, this was our daily regimen. You didn't question it. You just did it every day. To apply this style into your repertory is truly to know how to dance forever. I know that Deb's intention is to give you a gift. Her goal for this book is to guide you toward understanding the craft, look, and attitude of the Fosse technique of dance.

Ben Vereen

Prologue

"In fifty years or so, it's gonna change, you know . . ."

The phrase comes from "Nowadays," one of John Kander and Fred Ebb's indelible songs for the enduring Bob Fosse hit *Chicago.* In the show, it refers to the wild social and sexual freedoms of the 1920s, when the story is set, with the extra layer of amusement that *Chicago* opened in 1975, during an era at least as wild and socially permissive as the Roaring Twenties. For people who love dancing, it has an extra layer of meaning as well: except in the cases of a handful of choreographers, dances inevitably change over half a decade, much less half a century. The technique becomes eroded or reconfigured for new generations of performers, the reasons for it become misconstrued, and the meanings of its theatrical context are forgotten.

Bob Fosse is one of those rare exceptions. Taskmaster though he was, his dancers adored both him and his work, and they refuse to permit the distortions to it brought about by entropy and forgetfulness without a fight. This book, by Debra McWaters, is an example of such devotion. The steps, gestures, and choreographic figures here, with their pristine isolations of body parts and irrepressible sensuality, represent only a portion of the full dance language that Fosse employed over the course of his four-decade-long career as a professional choreographer for Broadway, Hollywood, and television. For, over time, Fosse called on jumps and lifts from classical ballet, ballroom, and character dance and knee slides, tumbling, and acrobatics from popular entertainment—big, full-bodied actions—as well as tap and soft shoe. "Sing, Sing, Sing!" the bravura number from his 1978 Broadway revue *Dancin'* (revived for the 1999 tribute revue *Fosse*), incorporated the full range of his dance vocabulary, and it is much larger than most theatergoers I know tend to recall without the memory aids of film and video.

Fosse also invented unique dance-theater movement for specific characters, as in the actions particular to each team member in his "Shoeless Joe" ballet in *Damn Yankees.* And, for some numbers, such as "Big Spender" in the 1966 *Sweet Charity* and "Mein Herr" in the 1972 film of *Cabaret,* his staging of groups of singer-dancers who are more or less rooted in space (the taxi dancers at a bar, the cabaret dancers on chairs) is so full of compressed kinetic energy that one has the impression they are dancing, even when they're frozen in place, cocking a snoot, so to speak, with an insinuating foot. Paradoxically, his dances connect with and excite audiences because the very austere technical requirements that restrict the dancer's body, in a way suggestive of psychological or cultural repression, also stimulate performers to open up their spirits; even when they're impersonating liars and crooks, they lead the audience to fall in love with them. The cooler the choreography and the more flawed the characters, the hotter the dancers.

So what you'll find full strength in these pages is the essence of the "Fosse style"—the catlike look of winking seduction and deeply ironic deliberation, as if the cat has just swallowed the canary—that immediately identifies a dancer as a member of a Fosse show. Influenced by vaudeville, burlesque, the demimonde of taxi dancers and sex shows, the distancing techniques of Bertolt Brecht, certain imagery in the leotard ballets of George Balanchine (which Fosse saw when the New York City Ballet performed at City Center and he lived across the street), and other aspects of theater in which sex and vulnerability consort with humor and cynicism, Fosse seems to have discovered the sensual streak in each of them and braided them all into a vision of theater and social politics that is distinctly his own.

It is a vision that depends on iron discipline: the dancing Fosse body, strictly designed by technique and choreography, is the product of inexhaustible repetitions in pursuit of mastery, and there are many stories by dancers and colleagues about how Fosse drove himself even harder than he drove them. Stanley Donen, the director of movie musicals and a former dancer, described Fosse's dance style in an interview with me for the *New York Times* in 1998, just prior to the local opening of the revue *Fosse:* "It's hard-edged," he said. "It's real. It's earthy. It's dynamic. It's extraordinarily theatrical. It's very American, full of unique movement. Its movements are small and very meaningful, in contrast to violent moods—the way he uses the hand, the way he holds his hat, with the wrist against the forehead, the fingers just so. Fosse thrived on what other people call awkward positions; his are wonderful and full of style. He was all detail. His dancers don't come out and smile at the audience, either. He imparts an attitude for each particular moment of dance. [He] was a great, great, great artist."

The emphasis in his movement on isolations of joints and appendages may recall the exuberant Charleston by dancers in films of African American revues from the 1920s, or the high-energy jazz dance of Matt Maddox from the 1950s, or the fluently multicultural dance language of Jack Cole, the choreographer who served as the first mentor of Gwen Verdon, beloved muse to Fosse and one of Broadway's greatest musical stars. Yet these isolations and jazz moves in Fosse's best-known dances are not spontaneously expressive and ranging in space but rather constructed and confined; it's part of Fosse's dance humor that they are, and the audience is meant to be in on the joke. Frequently, the struts, shoulder undulations, pelvic rotations, and cockatoo displays of the fingers seem to be squeezed out at half the tempo of the music; the silent-movie effect includes an element of the sinister, which points up the dark humor that results when theatrical illusion is harnessed to unseemly intentions, as it is, for example, in the plot of *Chicago*. The discrepancy between movement and music also exaggerates the shapes the body makes in profile, increasing their fascination for their own sake, outside a dramatic context.

And in some of Fosse's darkest choreography from the 1970s—for his narrator in *Pippin*, his vamps in *Chicago*, his cavorting female band in the film of *Cabaret*—one glimpses German Expressionist antecedents. "Bob was very influenced by Bertolt Brecht and Kurt Weill," the Fosse muse Ann Reinking said, when interviewed for the *Times* about her participation as a coach for *Fosse*. "That huge type of creativity which takes nothing and makes it into something very wrenching. The one thing I wanted to do was to create an air of quiet mystery. Fosse would say that it's important to trust silence. He very much liked the use of the tacit, or silent, count, where nothing is happening. He also liked percussion. His is a world of angular movement and mystery, quiet, semi-taciturn and percussive. I wanted to draw people into his world." Reinking's observation puts a dance historian in mind, too, of the silent mechanical isolations of the Death figure and of the tiptoeing catwalk by the derby-hatted and gloved Profiteer in *The Green Table*, the 1932 landmark of German Expressionist dance, by Kurt Jooss. Fosse easily could have seen it in New York during the 1970s, as the Joffrey Ballet had it in its repertory in a staging by Jooss himself, although Fosse might also have come in contact with it indirectly, through colleagues who had seen it, either in the 1970s or the 1930s, or through films.

Perhaps more important than the dance context, though, is the political one that was obtained in the United States when *Cabaret*, *Pippin*, and *Chicago* were conceived and developed. It was a period overshadowed by the Vietnam War, with its blatant governmental lying that fooled almost no one, and by the Watergate break-in, which led to the jaw-dropping, real-life circus of revelations and impeachment proceedings. Audiences arrived at the theater already cynical, and what they saw on stage in these shows mirrored that cynicism while also providing delicious entertainment. Fosse's conjunction of theatrical illusion with political hypocrisy was hardly new to him in the late 1960s and 1970s: in 1961, as the first choreographer hired for *The Conquering Hero*—a musical based on the 1944 Preston Sturges film, *Hail the Conquering Hero*—he staged a ballet cartoon of a battle between preening, golden American marines, played by men, and fierce, un-self-regarding Japanese warriors, played by women, a concept ahead of its time and for which he was fired before the show opened. (Even without him, it lasted only a week or so before closing down.) Still, the era of the Vietnam War and Watergate harmonized perfectly with Fosse's outlook on the relationship between life and show business.

Finally, Charlie Chaplin's Little Tramp is also part of the Fosse style. Fosse admired Chaplin, perhaps more, even, than he admired Fred Astaire, and his friends and colleagues have noted the Chaplinesque aspect of the derby hats, the white gloves, the canes, and the combination of short-gaited walks and vulnerable personalities in many of Fosse's dancing figures—a combo first found, says former Fosse dancer and chronicler Margery Beddow, in his show-stopping "Steam Heat" trio from *The Pajama Game* of 1956. Fosse's own abilities and limitations as a dancer seemed, to many who knew him, to be summarized and transfigured in this Chaplinesque aspect of his work. In 1974, with his typical candor, he spoke of himself as "being involved in something . . . called Eccentric dancing," a term that was used in vaudeville and cabaret as a classification for performers (usually comic ones) whose sources for steps were eclectic and whose execution of movement was idiosyncratic. "Eccentric" also means off-center, of course, and in some of Fosse's choreography one sees that idea literally embodied, as in walks or struts where the pelvis leads, or in asymmetrical isolations or poses.

And yet, for an eccentric, he managed to showcase and glorify the dancing and acting of many dancers who, unlike him, were thoroughly trained in classical ballet, modern dance, and/or jazz—Gwen Verdon, Ann Reinking, Ben Vereen, Chita Rivera, for starters. Edward Liang, the choreographer and dancer with the New York City Ballet, looks like a god in the 2002 Channel Thirteen/WNET New York documentary of the recent posthumous tribute revue, *Fosse*—a labor of love for a decade on the part of the dancer and choreographer Chet Walker, who had proposed it to Fosse himself before the latter's death from a heart attack in 1987, and then impressed Verdon into service by the results of workshops and classes he had run in the Fosse repertory, leading Verdon to reach out to Reinking to join the project. "There are so many facets to this choreography and to its vocabulary of movement," Verdon said in her *Times* interview. "It's funny. It's sexy. It's quick. It's romantic. There's so much detail. And you have such a sense of accomplishment—when you're finally able to accomplish it." She added, "When I did *Redhead*, which played in New York for 22 months and then toured, only six performances came together. Six! Performances when I sang well and danced well. When I did it right."

Mindy Aloff

Quotations from "A Loving Celebration of All That's Fosse," by Mindy Aloff, *New York Times*, September 13, 1998, copyright 1998 by The New York Times Company, reprinted by permission.

Acknowledgments

The writing in this book is mine. The knowledge presented between the covers, however, was passed on to me by some of the legends in this industry.

It is most obvious that I owe a debt of gratitude to the education in the Fosse style passed on to me by Ann Reinking. My travels with Gwen Verdon allowed me to fill my journal with priceless information about Bob Fosse's work. There is not a day that goes by when thoughts of Gwen do not bring a smile to my face. Ben Vereen, my dear friend and inspiration, continues to fill my head with information on the style of Mr. Fosse, my heart with happiness, and my soul with spirit. He has encouraged me to "stay in the heights." The stories Chita Rivera shared with me about her experiences working with Mr. Fosse added both substance and nuance to my knowledge of his work. Working with Bebe Neuwirth and Joel Grey in the revival of *Chicago* exposed subtleties of this technique for which I am truly grateful.

It is impossible to think of Bob Fosse without thinking of John Kander and Fred Ebb. The experience of working with these two legends is something that remains a dream to me. Fred has left us, but John continues to spread love and music throughout the world.

Between working on *Chicago* and *Fosse*, I have had the privilege of interacting with many stunning dancers who worked with Fosse while he was alive: Kathryn Doby, frequent dance captain, Sandahl Bergman, Cheryl Clark, Lloyd Culbreath, Christine Colby, John Mineo, Michael Kubala, Jeff Shade, Bruce Anthony Davis, Stephanie Pope, Kim Morgan Greene, Jane Lanier, Dana Moore, Valarie Pettiford, David Warren-Gibson, and William Whitener. I apologize to any whose names I have left off this list.

I am deeply grateful to the Broadway Theatre Project for its efforts to continue to train musical theatre students and to teach them how to be the best in the field while becoming healthy and well-rounded human beings. The Project allows the Fosse style to be taught in depth and has turned out many a cast member for a Fosse musical. I cannot mention Broadway Theatre Project without thanking Kim Slade, Program Director, for supporting my efforts in any way she could.

I have been fortunate to work with Meredith Morris-Babb, director of University Press of Florida, who asked me to write this book and supported me during each step of the process. Her tenacity in reaching me during my travels is very much appreciated.

Tom Porter has made this book come alive with his stunning photographs and his collaborative spirit. The subjects of these beautiful pictures—Nicole Baker, Noel Becker, Zane Booker, and Ashley Fitzgerald—reached into their memory banks and pulled out their knowledge of this technique in order to enable the reader to see how the work should be done. These four dancers graced one of the *Fosse* companies, and I have never been more grateful than for their participation in the making of this book. Darren Lorenzo deserves thanks for his invaluable help to me throughout the photographic process. I owe a debt of gratitude to the Patel Conservatory at the Tampa Bay Performing Arts Center for so generously supplying us with a space for photographing.

A special debt of thanks is owed to Don Jones for his spectacular photographs of Ben Vereen and the author. The pictures of the author would not have been possible without the help of Broadmoor Fire Protection District, Allison Scott of the Broadmoor hotel, and Don Jones's technical support team.

I thank the producers from NAMCO, ClearChannel, and Networks for entrusting me with their many companies of *Chicago* and *Fosse*. I wish to voice my appreciation to Darren Gibson and Fabian Aloise who, with their endless enthusiasm, excellent technique, and eye for detail, took the word *assistant* to a new level.

My brother, Randy, his family, and my mother and father continue to cheer me on during my creative efforts. I am the most fortunate woman alive.

Finally, I must thank my husband, Marcus, for standing by me throughout our lives and for encouraging me to "gather ye rosebuds while ye may."

Introduction

Writing a book on the style of the Tony, Emmy, and Academy Award–winning legend, director-choreographer Bob Fosse, is truly a privilege. There is no question that this man was a genius, and out of this genius came the birth of a style of dance that is whimsical, sensuous, and recognizable by almost anyone who has an interest in the arts. With the success of the revival of *Chicago* and *Fosse*, the style is having a resurgence, and both instructors and dancers are desiring to implement Fosse-like movement in their work.

What this book is going to attempt to accomplish is in-depth descriptions as well as photographs of dancers well trained in the Fosse style. The dancers selected—Nicole Baker, Noel Becker, Zane Booker, and Ashley Fitzgerald—performed in the musical *Fosse*, and had the privilege of gleaning information from Gwen Verdon and Ben Vereen. They are all either faculty members or alumni of the most prestigious musical theatre training program in the United States, the Broadway Theatre Project. Each

Noel Becker

Zane Booker

Nicole Baker and Ashley Fitzgerald

dancer is adept at many styles of dance, and each has learned how to bring acting to their craft.

The book is divided into three sections related first with the individual parts of the body and various Fosse moves associated with those parts, then with combinations of these isolated areas into steps and movement. Last, I have choreographed a combination in the Fosse style that should help the dancer to actually place what was learned from reading the book into his or her body.

Included in the descriptions throughout the book is the addition of various images that Bob Fosse related to his dancers in order to aid in the teaching of his style. This is precious information, as it was passed from Fosse to Gwen Verdon, Ann Reinking, Ben Vereen, Chita Rivera, and Liza Minnelli, among others. During my time working with Ann Reinking, Gwen Verdon, and Ben Vereen, I was privileged to learn of the different images used to inspire the dancers and add clarification to Bob Fosse's choreography. This is the epitome of the passing down of information in order to keep an art form alive.

My hope with this book is that this information will now be passed down to another generation of dancers and they will be able to dance the style in an informed and correct manner. Keeping this work alive is a goal for many, and I hope that this book will help in doing so.

1

Hands

As distinctive as the hunched shoulders, turned-in legs, and arms akimbo are the many positions that the hands sequence through while dancing in the Fosse vernacular. Several of the positions or movements will look familiar, but others are not as commonplace to those who are new to the look of the Fosse style.

Positions

Splayed Fingers

The fingers are stretched and separated from one another. One might find splayed fingers resting on the hipbones (figure 1.1) or covering the dome of a derby for a lovely pattern (figure 1.2), made all the more powerful by a long line of dancers all holding their derbies in the same fashion.

Figure 1.1

Figure 1.2

Faun Hands

This received its name from Nijinsky's hand positions in *Afternoon of a Faun*. The palm is flat and the fingers are extended, but unlike Splayed Fingers, they are close enough together that they touch. In this technique, Faun Hands usually break at an angle from the forearm and wrist (figures 1.3 and 1.4).

Figure 1.3

Figure 1.4

Blocking the Sun

This resembles Faun Hands in that the position is almost identical. The placement of the hand is above the head and lined up with an imaginary seam connecting the "wall" in front of the body with the "ceiling." The arm is slightly curved and the shoulder is down. The image is that of one blocking the sun from one's eyes (figure 1.5).

Figure 1.5

Saucer Hands

This occurs when the hands are placed at the hipbones, with the thumb extended and resting against the back of the body, right above the buttocks; the other four fingers of each hand are extended and touching, and the palms are parallel to the floor. The index fingers rest against the front of the body at the hipbone. The elbows are out in a pronounced fashion and there is power in the upper and lower arms as well as in the shoulders (figure 1.6).

Figure 1.6

Soft-Boiled-Egg Hands

This is perhaps one of the most commonly used descriptors of a Fosse move. The hands are relaxed. All five fingers are bent and curled as if cautiously carrying a soft-boiled egg. The thumb is positioned in such a way that it rests lightly against the third and fourth fingers. There should be no gripping of the fingers to the palm. The sensation should be loose (figure 1.7).

Figure 1.7

Teacup Fingers

This may be one of the most popular and best known of the Fosse hand positions. One simply touches the tips of the thumb and the forefinger together so that a circle or an oval is formed (figure 1.8). The remaining three fingers are splayed. The image is similar to the hand position one might have when holding a cup of tea. This position is frequently used when a derby is part of the costuming for a particular number (figure 1.9).

Figure 1.8

Figure 1.9

East Indian Hands

Fosse was greatly influenced by the work of Jack Cole, and this influence can be seen occasionally in Fosse's work. These hands are executed by pinching the thumb and middle finger together. The forearms are turned so that the elbows point down toward the floor and the plane of the forearms is almost parallel to the plane of the floor. The remaining fingers are separated (figure 1.10).

Figure 1.10

Placement

Draped at Waist

The hands hang loosely from bent wrists and are placed at waist level, flush with the body. The elbows are bent and point toward the back. The forearms are angled toward the floor or are parallel to the plane of the floor and remain very close to the sides of the torso (figures 1.19 and 1.20).

Figure 1.11

Figure 1.12

On Ribs or Back

There are various possibilities for using the hands in one of these positions. Basically, the palms are placed somewhere on the side of the rib cage or high up on the back with the arms bent and elbows prominently sticking out. The oddness of this look comes from the placement of the hands high up on the rib cage, rather than at waist or hip level (figure 1.13).

Figure 1.13

Wrists

Wrist Curls with Fists

This is simply an isolation. The hands are in a soft fist, and the wrists are loose enough to move in a smooth circular fashion. There should be an attempt to keep the remainder of the arm still (figures 1.14 and 1.15).

Figure 1.14

Figure 1.15

Wrist Curls with Opening Fingers

Again, this is an isolation. The hands begin in a soft fist; the wrists are loose and again move in a smooth circular fashion. This time, as the wrist circles, the fingers, beginning with the pinkie, open and straighten sequentially and then curl back into a fist. Again, there should be an attempt to keep the remainder of the arm still (figures 1.16 through 1.18). It is very important to articulate the fingers as much as possible in order to do this hand movement correctly.

Figure 1.16

Figure 1.17

Figure 1.18

Isolated Wrist with Finger Snaps

In this movement, the upper arm and forearm are kept still as the hand hangs from the wrist. The wrist isolates by bending so that the hand moves toward the ceiling. At the height of this movement, the fingers snap. Nothing else moves (figures 1.19 through 1.21). As the isolation reverses, the hand moves in a downward direction and there is no snap. The sequence moves continuously.

Figure 1.19

Figure 1.20

Figure 1.21

Moves

Cranking at the Hip

This motion is one that appears relatively easy but, in fact, is rather difficult to execute exactly as Mr. Fosse desired. Ben Vereen relates that during the rehearsals for "Rich Man's Frug" from *Sweet Charity*, the movement, which also involves other parts of the body in the number and which will be discussed later, was rehearsed for an entire day.

To begin with, the hands are in Soft-Boiled-Egg position. Each hand is flush against the matching hipbone. The arms are parallel to each other, but both are bent at the elbow. The knuckles are facing in a downward direction toward the floor, and the wrists are bent.

The hands move in a circle. The motion begins as the wrists move upward bringing the knuckles to face the direction in which the dancer is facing. The knuckles are now in line with the wrist. At this point the elbows, still bent, are spaced considerably away from the back. The heels of the hands are pushing back behind the dancer, but the inside of the fist remains next to the hipbone (figures 1.22 and 1.23). The entire motion is done repeatedly, with a slight hesitation as the heels of the hands push back.

Figure 1.22   Figure 1.23

Monkey

Here, I am only going to describe the motion of the hands in a step to be described later called Monkey Down. The hands are in Soft-Boiled-Egg position, the left at eye level, the right at mid-torso level. At the beginning of the movement, both sets of knuckles are facing the direction in which the dancer is facing (figure 1.24).

Once the Monkey Down begins, the hands begin to alternate. Both wrists are cocked and the knuckles of both hands are facing opposite directions: the knuckles of the left hand face the ceiling and the knuckles of the right hand face the floor. The upper arms are parallel to the plane of the floor and make right angles with the forearms (figure 1.25). As the hands change place, the motion is nice and tight. It is never a large, ungainly movement. It should be thought of as being contained.

Figure 1.24

Figure 1.25

Window Washer

This occurs in front of the torso. The hands are flat, and the palms face out or toward the audience. The fingers are either splayed or together. The elbows are bent, and the arms and hands can be fairly close to the body (see figures 1.26 through 1.28), or they can move farther away from the torso (figures 1.29 through 1.32).

The move is fluid and goes from right to left or left to right. The hands, leading with the heels, initiate the movement, always keeping the same relative distance from each other. The forearms move only because the hands are moving. The image is that of having rags in both hands and wiping a window with both hands simultaneously. A slight arc is etched in space as the movement is executed.

Figure 1.26

Figure 1.27

Figure 1.28

Figure 1.29

Figure 1.30

Figure 1.31

Figure 1.32

2

Arms

As the discussion moves from the hands to the arms, in many cases one finds the execution of a move that heavily involves the hands. Reference will frequently be made to the hand positions from chapter 1.

In many examples of port de bras (carriage of the arms) in the Fosse style, the sequence is initiated by the elbow, followed by the wrist and then the hand. In essence, what occurs is that the elbow bends; as it begins to straighten the wrist begins to flex; once the arm is straight and the wrist is flexed, the hand extends. The following illustrations of port de bras closely explain how the sequence of elbow, wrist, and hand is important in the Fosse vernacular (figures 2.1 through 2.19). Gwen Verdon explained that as the hand extends, the dancers should think of a feather being gently released into the air (figures 2.20 through 2.22). It is a lovely description.

Figure 2.1

Figure 2.2

Figure 2.3

Figure 2.4

Figure 2.7

Figure 2.8

Figure 2.5

Figure 2.6

Figure 2.9

Figure 2.10

Figure 2.13

Figure 2.14

Figure 2.11

Figure 2.12

Figure 2.15

Figure 2.16

Figure 2.17

Figure 2.20

Figure 2.21

Figure 2.18

Figure 2.19

Figure 2.22

Broken Doll Arms

In chapter 1 we discussed Splayed Fingers, which will be used in this position. The upper arms are straight and located slightly away from the trunk of the body. The elbows are pointing downward. There is a break at the elbows, and the forearms are held either parallel to the plane of the floor or at a slight angle. The fingers of both hands are splayed (figure 2.23). It is important to note that there are variations of Broken Doll, which will be explained in more detail later.

Figure 2.23

Piston Arms

The hands are flexed, the elbows point toward the audience, the arms are close to the torso, and the palms are parallel to the plane of the floor. The fingertips are pointing upstage. As one arm bends completely at the elbow with the arms and hands remaining in position, the other arm is straight down by the side of the body with the hand flexed in a similar fashion. Then the arms switch positions at the same time (figures 2.24 and 2.25). This is repeated to give the impression of pistons moving up and down.

Figure 2.24

Figure 2.25

Sable Brushes

In a sense, this is similar to Piston Arms, as the arms move alternately and repetitively. Sable Brush arms are quite beautiful, however, as one imagines sable paint brushes stroking the sides of the body—up and down. When the "brush" is moving down the body, the elbow is completely bent and pointing away from the body. The hand is soft, and the fingertips slightly curled inward so that the nails are touching the side of the body. The fingers softly move down the body.

At the same time the opposite is happening with the other hand. This arm originates in a downward position with the fingertips facing the floor. As it begins its upward journey, the elbows point away from the torso and the fingertips lightly brush the body as the hands move up from the thigh to right below the armpit. The fingertips are not slightly curled (figures 2.26 and 2.27).

Figure 2.26

Figure 2.27

Fosse Arms

So much has been made of Fosse Arms, including Robin Williams's wonderful and comedic summary of dance styles in *The Birdcage*. The crucial thing to remember when doing this movement is that it always initiates with the elbow, then moves to the wrist and finally to the hand. This sequence was mentioned in the first section of this chapter. Note that the dancers in the illustrations are facing US. All references to positioning will pertain to this initial orientation. Therefore, the use of SR and SL will pertain to the dancer's true reference to right and left as he or she faces the audience. The hands can be open softly or in Soft-Boiled-Egg position. The arms work in unison, not alternating.

In order to do this port de bras correctly, both arms must be positioned behind the back. The motion begins with both elbows moving SR. The wrists of both hands flex toward SR (or SL if the movement is to begin in that direction). In this case, the left wrist is flexed so that the fingertips are pointing toward SL, the outside of the wrist is facing SR, and the inside of the right wrist is pointing toward SL, as are the fingertips. As the wrists flex, the arms are moving toward SR in a curved manner. Once the elbows have finished their movement to the right, the wrists flex in the opposite direction from where they were prior to this, the fingers extend softly, and the movement continues toward SL (figures 2.28 through 2.32).

This is a repetitive movement that should be done as if one is moving underwater. Think of being in the shallow end of a swimming pool, moving the water right and left with the fingers. It is also important to note that this movement is best done with the upper arms held fairly close to the torso.

Figure 2.28

Figure 2.29

Figure 2.31

Figure 2.30

Figure 2.32

Drop of Water

In this positioning of the arms, it is important to know that it is similar to the next position to be discussed, New York Times, yet there is a definite difference between the two. Here, the elbows are broken, the forearms are somewhat angled toward the floor, the wrists are broken, and the hands are "dripping": very relaxed with the fingertips pointing toward the floor. The upper arm is separated from the upper torso by several inches. Drop of Water comes from the image of a drop of water originating on the shoulder, rolling down the slope of the upper arm, down the forearm onto the hand, and off of the fingertips onto the floor (figures 2.33 and 2.34).

Figure 2.33

Figure 2.34

New York Times

As was mentioned above, this is similar to Drop of Water. The elbows are still bent, forearms are parallel to the plane of the floor, wrists are dripping, and hands are relaxed with fingertips pointing toward the floor. The difference is that the elbows do touch the sides of the body and the upper arms are held very close to the sides of the torso. The image is that of holding a *New York Times* under one's arm (figures 2.35 through 2.37).

Figure 2.35

Figure 2.36

Figure 2.37

Fur Coat

This is the phrase Gwen Verdon used to describe movement of the arms into a particular position. The arms are dangling loosely behind the back, straight and with the fingertips pointing toward the floor. Raise the hands, bringing the arms to shoulder height, with the inside of the forearms facing the ceiling. As they hit shoulder height, the wrists are flipped over so that the fingertips are now pointing downward, and the hands move down toward the floor as if putting one's arms through the sleeves of a very expensive fur coat. Note that the fingers are together as the arms move through the sleeves of the coat. The movement itself is done with several inches of space between the arms and the body. The ending position is the same as the initial position (figures 2.38 through 2.42).

Figure 2.38

Figure 2.39

Figure 2.40

Figure 2.41

Figure 2.42

Scooping Sugar

Typically a hat is held in the working hand. For the purposes of description here, a derby will be used. Holding the hat by the brim, dome facing out, make an arc with the working arm, allowing the derby to continue around in a circle with the arms softly bent until it is in front of the chest, dome facing out, and both hands are holding opposite sides of the hat by the brim. Note that when the motion begins, the hat never passes in front of the face. Also, until the opposite hand grabs the brim, that hand is on the hipbone, elbow out, fingers splayed (figures 2.43 through 2.47).

Figure 2.43

Figure 2.44

Figure 2.45

Figure 2.46

Figure 2.47

Curved Arms behind Back

In this position, the arms are behind the back with several inches separating them from the back. They are curved, parallel to each other, and the fingertips are pointing toward the ground (figures 2.48 through 2.50).

Figure 2.48

Figure 2.49

Figure 2.50

Birdie Wings

I always enjoyed hearing Gwen Verdon refer to this position as Birdie Wings. She used to enjoy describing these movements as those belonging to baby birds.

To place the arms in the appropriate position, the hands are flat on either side of the hipbones. The fingers are close together on the hips in order to hold on tightly. The elbows move so that they are pointing toward the back, and there is strong energy in the arms as they pin the elbows in that position. The forearms are pinned against the sides of the body. If one looks at this position from the side, it resembles bird wings (figure 2.51).

In figure 2.52, Noel's arms are bent, with forearms angled downward, upper arms away from the torso. Seen live, the fingers are "dancing." This also gives the impression of a bird on the wing.

Figure 2.52

Figure 2.51

Arm Drape

This form falls in the category of familiar Fosse images. It can occur in a variety of ways, but I will describe one that is used frequently. One arm is raised, elbow bent, forearm resting on top of the head, wrist broken, and hand relaxed. The other arm might be doing a variety of other things, including matching the one I just described so that both arms are draped on the head. There are wonderful variations of arm drapes (figures 2.53 and 2.54).

Figure 2.53

Figure 2.54

3

Shoulders

The shoulders in this work are used as much as any other part of the body. There are two basic positions.

The Slouch

Frequently in Fosse's work, one can see slouching shoulders, meaning that there is a sense of a droop. It is almost as if one is looking at a suit hanging crookedly on a

Figure 3.1

hanger. One very typical example occurs by slightly rolling the shoulders forward and raising one shoulder while lowering the other so that they almost appear to be on a diagonal. This is typically accompanied by a similarly laconic pose using the lower body (figures 3.1 and 3.2). The entire position will be addressed later. Fosse said that his style came out of his "imperfections." The slouch is one of these, which developed out of his rounded posture.

Figure 3.2

Scissoring

The Broken Doll movement frequently employs Scissoring of the shoulders. (It also can occur with the shoulders kept perfectly still.) Scissoring of the shoulders is fairly easy to understand, as it is an isolation that involves one shoulder moving down sharply as the other simultaneously rises sharply toward the ear. As soon as that is accomplished, the movement reverses (figures 3.3 and 3.4). The move alternates and repeats.

Figure 3.3

Figure 3.4

4

Hips and Derrière

Back Bumps

Many people associate Fosse's work with hip and pelvic movements, although there is much more to it than that. The best way to describe these particular isolations is to break down what are called Back Bumps. There are many variations, but this section will deal with the basic move.

Start with feet together and knees straight. Tilt the pelvis slightly forward (figure 4.1), then plié, arch the back, and extend the derrière (figure 4.2). As the legs straighten, take the arch out of the back and tilt the pelvis slightly forward. Once the legs hit the straightened position, the back has arched once again and the derrière is extended (figure 4.3). Repeat. This movement is done continuously.

Figure 4.1

Figure 4.2

Figure 4.3

Dusting the Piano Bench

Gwen Verdon described this movement using this name, and it is a most accurate and enjoyable analogy. Stand with the feet in parallel second position (figure 4.4). Note that the dancers are facing US, and the directions will be given relative to that orientation. Plié and send the right hip toward SL (figure 4.5). Remain in plié and sweep the hips from SL to SR (figure 4.6). As the right hip ends its movement to the right, bring the right foot into the left foot, so that both are in parallel first position. Then straighten the legs and bring the hips back to neutral (figure 4.7).

Figure 4.4

Figure 4.5

Figure 4.6

Figure 4.7

Hip Swings

Stand with feet slightly apart and in parallel position. Plié and keep the center of gravity directly between the feet. Maintain this position and swing the hips toward SR and then toward SL (figures 4.8 and 4.9). Repeat continuously. While doing this, one can use Splayed Fingers as a variation.

Figure 4.8

Figure 4.9

5

Legs and Feet

Hook

Stand on one leg, lift the other in parallel position, turn the raised foot in, and then hook it behind the standing leg. The standing leg is usually in plié (figure 5.1).

Figure 5.1

Rond de Jambe with Wrist Curls

Extend one leg in front of the body with a soft knee. The standing leg is in plié. The toes of the extended leg are on the floor. The legs are parallel. The rond de jambe is very small and is accomplished by drawing small circles on the floor with the toes of the extended leg, while maintaining the level of the body in plié. At the same time the rond de jambe is occurring, the arms are extended in front of the body, parallel to the plane of the floor, with elbows slightly bent. The level of the hands is right beneath the eyes.

The hands execute Wrist Curls with Opening Fingers (described in chapter 1). The Wrist Curls and the rond de jambe occur at the same time (figures 5.2 through 5.6). Note that the Wrist Curls are in opposite directions of each other and move at the same rate as the foot drawing the circles.

Figure 5.2

Figure 5.3

Figure 5.4

Figure 5.5

Figure 5.6

Leg Switches

One can best view the body during this movement from the side. The step itself can be done facing any direction.

Begin with the left leg bent and the left set of toes touching the ground, heel up. The left foot should be near the instep of the right foot. The right leg is very straight. The feet are in parallel position. There is a slight arch in the back so that the derrière is not tucked under (figure 5.7).

Bring the hips underneath the body, the feet in relevé, while the legs switch (figure 5.8). Once they have reversed positions, the back is arched once again and the derrière is released (figure 5.9). Leg Switches are frequently paired with Back Bumps (described in chapter 4).

Figure 5.7   Figure 5.8   Figure 5.9

6

Walks

Forward Walks

Broken Doll

For this walk we will use Broken Doll Arms (described in chapter 2). The only addition is that the shoulders will Scissor. However, the walk can be done without the Scissoring. The feet are slightly turned in during this walk, but do not mistake this as a request for pigeon-toed feet. Many who have not been formally taught Fosse's style mistakenly turn in their feet to a great degree under the misconception that this is how the walk is accomplished. Gwen Verdon gave a wonderful analogy for learning how to move the feet when doing a Fosse Walk: "If a line is drawn on the floor, try to walk on it without falling off." Note that the feet are turned in only very slightly in order to accomplish this task (figures 6.1 and 6.2). This is the best way to learn how to do the walk that is seen so frequently in Fosse's work.

In the actual walk in this movement, each step is a large one. As the foot steps out, the weight transfers to it and the heel of the back leg rises in preparation for the next step. If the shoulders Scissor, the right shoulder drops and the left lifts as the right foot

Figure 6.1   Figure 6.2

steps forward (figure 6.3). Then the left shoulder drops and the right lifts as the left foot steps forward (figure 6.4). Repeat alternately and continuously (figure 6.5 shows Broken Doll without scissoring the shoulders).

Figure 6.3

Figure 6.4

Figure 6.5

Fosse Walk

This is a signature walk in the Fosse style. It appears to be easily executed, but in fact it is quite difficult to do correctly.

During the entire walking sequence, the Fosse Arms (described in chapter 2) will be used. The footwork is somewhat similar to that which was used in Broken Doll Walk. Once again, it is as if one is trying to walk on a line painted on the floor. The feet are slightly turned in, but only very slightly and only in order to keep the body on the imaginary line. The stride is much smaller than that used in Broken Doll, and the back heel does not pop as the front foot steps forward.

As a step is taken with the right foot, the arms undulate to the right. (Figures 6.6 and 6.7 show the walk with open hands; figures 6.8 and 6.9 show the walk with Soft-Boiled-Egg hands.) Remember that the sequence for moving the arms is always elbows first, then wrists, and finally hands. Repeat continuously.

Figure 6.6

Figure 6.7

Figure 6.8

Figure 6.9

Xs and Os

This is a movement that is more difficult to execute than one would expect, but when done correctly, it appears that the dancer is moving effortlessly across the floor.

Begin the movement in a very loose fifth position, right foot front (figure 6.10). The first effort is to push off with the ball of the right foot and move to a pigeon-toed position in relevé with the knees turned in so that a knock-kneed look is achieved (figure 6.11). Return to the starting position. Repeat, but move to the toed-in position in plié. The legs and feet move at a rapid rate, but the upper body is absolutely still. This can be accomplished, however, only if the level of the body never changes. (Figures 6.12 and 6.13 show another version of Xs and Os.)

Figure 6.10

Figure 6.11

Figure 6.12

Figure 6.13

Durantes

Start with legs in second position with feet parallel. The legs are absolutely straight. The body is curved back so that the pelvis is forward. There is no forced arch in the back, however. The arms hang behind the back. They appear to be loose but have a slight curve; a definite energy is evident.

In order to do a Durante, step with the right foot so that the foot barely leaves the floor, stays flat, and digs into the floor. The left foot then does the same thing. Repeat continuously (figures 6.14 and 6.15). Add a "head bobble." The head bobbles on the neck loosely like the toys with heads on springs. (Figure 6.16 shows the movement as seen in "Steam Heat" from *Fosse*.)

This step is called the Durante because the famous entertainer of the 1950s, Jimmy Durante, used to exit his show this way. He was a lovable television personality with a bulbous nose and a gravelly voice, and this walk was one of his signature moves.

Figure 6.14

Figure 6.15

Figure 6.16

Step Together with Hip Circle

Begin with the feet together. Step to the right onto the ball of the right foot and let the heel gently lower to the floor. As the weight goes to the right ball, the right hip is slightly lifted, and it circles in a clockwise direction. Once the weight has transferred to the right ball, the left foot moves to the right foot and the weight changes to the left foot.

One way to execute this smooth movement is to allow the left hand to droop from the waist. The right hand does Wrist Curls with Opening Fingers (described in chapter 2). The wrist is near the right hipbone. The focus is down toward the right foot (figures 6.17 through 6.19). There are many variations of this step (figures 6.20 through 6.22).

Figure 6.17

Figure 6.18

Figure 6.19

Figure 6.20

Figure 6.21

Figure 6.22

Hip Roll Walk

For this walk the arms can be held either up with the wrists "dripping" (described in chapter 2, Drop of Water) or behind the back and curved. Begin by stepping on the ball of the right foot and adding a clockwise hip circle with the right hip. As the hip circle is completed, the left foot takes the weight. This walk repeats the one above. It takes two counts to execute one complete step (figures 6.23 through 6.25).

Figure 6.23

Figure 6.24

Figure 6.25

Bicycle

This resembles Groucho Marx's walk in the old Marx Brothers' movies. For this walk, stay in plié, pick up the knees as a step is taken, and keep the feet flat. An interesting way in which to use the Bicycle is to allow the hands to be held in the East Indian position (described in chapter 1). The arms are bent at the elbow and the hands are to the right and left of the body, respectively (figures 6.26 through 6.32).

Figure 6.26

Figure 6.27

Figure 6.28

Figure 6.29

Figure 6.30

Figure 6.31

Figure 6.32

Sugars

The place where this walk is quite evident in Fosse's work is in the number "Sing Sing Sing" from the musical *Dancin'* and it most recently was seen in the musical *Fosse*. It is a very "cool" step that is beautifully married to the Bennie Goodman music to which it is performed.

To begin, think of having on a corset that is very tight. Pull the torso up and bend over slightly, but you can only go so far because of the tightness. Allow the arms to dangle down in front of the body. Relevé on both feet, soften both knees, and step on the right foot, toes pointing toward the right as far as possible. While the right foot is executing this, the left foot swivels right. Then step on the left foot with toes pointing left as far as possible. The right foot swivels on the ball to the left. The focus is toward the floor during this entire movement. The upper body remains stationary as the footwork is executed (figures 6.33 and 6.34).

Figure 6.33

Figure 6.34

Sneakies

This movement was used in "Fosse's World" in *Fosse* and is another step from the ver-nacular. The Fosse team gave this walk its name because the entire idea is to make it appear that you are "sneaking" across the stage on tiptoe. As can be seen in the illustra-tions, the walk goes from the right foot to the left foot repeatedly. Both legs are slightly bent. The torso is bent over, and there is a slight contraction in the midsection. The shoulders are raised. The focus is toward the floor, and the US hand is holding the front brim of the derby with Teacup Fingers. The left arm moves forward and back with elbows softly bent. That hand is in the Soft-Boiled-Egg position.

As you step on the ball of the right foot, the left arm swings forward; it swings backward as you step on the ball of the left foot. Note that as the left hand moves backward, the wrist flexes so that the heel of the hand is pushing backward (figures 6.35 through 6.38).

Figure 6.35

Figure 6.36

Figure 6.37

Figure 6.38

Lolas

This step got its name from the character who danced it, Lola, in the Fosse musical *Damn Yankees*. It was also done in the revival of *Chicago* and in *Fosse*.

Start on the balls of both feet. The feet are slightly turned in, and the legs are together. The backs of the wrists of the hands are touching, and the fingers are in East Indian position. The arms are softly bent.

As a step is taken, the foot moves slightly in front of the other foot. The step is extremely small. One leg crosses just slightly in front of the other. The shoulders may remain up or may move upward and downward on one step and the same on the next step, in which case the count is [and, 1], with the [1] occurring as the ball of the foot hits the ground. It can be done either way (figures 6.39 and 6.40). This is yet another Fosse step that is very whimsical.

Figure 6.39

Figure 6.40

Backward Walks

Basic

These walks are an interesting use of the style to execute something that has a strong visual impact (figure 6.41).

Begin by executing an undulating walk backward, toward the audience. The positioning of the arms can vary, but the footwork is the same. The feet are slightly turned in, and as you step backward with the right foot, the outside of the foot drags lightly on the floor and an arc is traced with it (figure 6.42). As the weight transfers to the right foot, the right leg is straightened (figure 6.43). Repeat the movement on the left foot and then again on the right (figures 6.44 through 6.47). When the weight reaches the right foot on the third repetition, execute a slow and soft pelvic thrust forward and then back to neutral. The upper torso does not shift as the steps are taken.

So far, the walk has been illustrated without using the shoulders. To add them, the same shoulder as the working foot rolls back (figures 6.48 and 6.49). Note in the pictures two of the possible arm positions used by the dancers in the number.

Figure 6.41

Figure 6.42

Figure 6.43

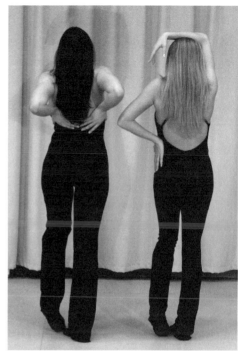

Figure 6.44

Figure 6.47

Figure 6.48

Figure 6.45

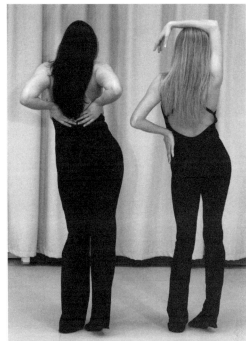

Figure 6.46

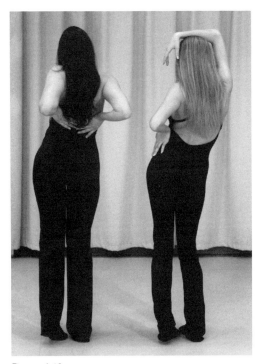

Figure 6.49

Susie Q

This can be seen in "Hot Honey Rag" from the 2007 Broadway version of *Chicago*. The step is normally done fairly rapidly. It is actually quite easy to execute but can be fairly difficult to learn because body parts are moving in different directions. It takes concentration while learning it to get each part moving in the correct direction before moving on to the next part and ultimately connecting all of the parts. Here it will be broken down.

Beginning with the feet, facing SR, initiate the step with the left leg. Pick the left foot up slightly so that the knee is bent and turned in, with the foot behind the body. The knees should practically be touching. This is on the count [and]. The foot then moves to the front of the body, and the heel hits the ground with the toes up, and it swivels quickly so that the toes are angled toward the audience on [1]. On [and], the toes move toward the right. On [2], the heel swivels so that the toes move to the left and lower to the floor as the weight shifts to the left leg. The left leg is in plié. Also

Figure 6.50

on [2], once the weight shift has been accomplished, the right foot comes up and the foot and leg take the same position as the left did above, only in the opposite direction. Repeat the step on the opposite leg. Note that the standing leg is always straight during the heel swivels.

Moving to the upper torso, on the first [and], it is twisted to the left, on [1], it twists to the right, on [and], it twists to the left, and on [2], it twists to the right.

Last is the arms. Begin with the arms up in front of the chest. The hands are in the East Indian position, with thumbs pinching third fingers, and palms facing downward. The hands are fairly close together, and the elbows are up and pointing right and left. It is perhaps clearer to say that, in general, the arms and torso move in opposite directions (figures 6.50 through 6.53). Note that on [2], as the working foot is moving from the heel to the entire bottom of the foot, the torso and the arms freeze in their positions until the next count.

Figure 6.51

Figure 6.52

Figure 6.53

Cake Walk

This walk also appears in "Hot Honey Rag" in *Chicago*. Facing SL, step back on the left foot, tendu with the right foot toward SL, and twist the torso toward DS. The arms are extended and bent at the elbows, the hands with Splayed Fingers. When the right foot is in tendu, the left arm is reaching upward and the right arm is reaching downward. The arms are almost on a diagonal (figure 6.54).

To continue, step back on the right foot and tendu with the left foot toward SL, twisting the torso toward US. Now the right arm is reaching upward, and the left arm is reaching downward (figure 6.55).

All the while, the hands are shaking and the steps are moving backward rapidly. At times, the step is so rapid that the tendu is done with slightly bent knees.

Figure 6.54

Figure 6.55

7

Body Positions

Hieroglyphic Stance

This stance may be used in a variety of ways. Basically, it is a position that makes you appear to be two-dimensional. When first executing a pose of this type, it may feel awkward, but as with anything practiced frequently, it will soon feel very natural. Here is one such stance.

To begin, face US, feet in a wide parallel fourth position with the left foot forward and legs in plié. The body is bent over slightly at the waist, the upper torso faces US, and the focus is toward the left foot. The right hand is in Teacup Fingers position and is holding the back brim of the derby. The elbow is lifted. The left hand is in Saucer position. The entire body is in the same plane, as if pressed between two boards. If this placement is done correctly, the image is of a two-dimensional figure that is hieroglyphic in nature (figure 7.1; see figures 7.2 through 7.4 for other examples).

Figure 7.1

Figure 7.2

Figure 7.3

Figure 7.4

Fred Astaire Foot

When this foot position is referred to, it is because the image conjures up memories of the many times Fred Astaire was seen in it. As a side note, Fosse was an avid fan of Astaire.

Begin with the left foot turned out and the left leg in a low plié. The right leg is behind the left and is extended toward stage left. The leg is straight and the right foot is rolled over so that the outside of the foot is on the floor. The ankle is broken to a great degree in order for this to be accomplished (figure 7.5). Different body positions may use a Fred Astaire Foot (figures 7.6 through 7.8). Note that in figure 7.7, the bodies are in hieroglyphic placement.

Figure 7.5

Figure 7.6

Figure 7.7

Figure 7.8

Bandit

This is a beautiful position. The image given by Gwen Verdon is that of a dusty bandit in the hills with a kerchief covering the nose and mouth, leaving only the eyes visible. The left foot is turned out, and the leg is in a deep plié. The right foot is in the Fred Astaire position. The torso is facing the audience. The left arm is extended to the left at shoulder height. The right arm is bent at the elbow, the elbow is lifted, and the lower portion of the forearm is in front of the face, covering the nose and mouth, so that only the eyes are visible (figure 7.9).

Figure 7.9

Turned-In Stance

There is a stance seen over and over again in Fosse's work. He said that he was naturally hunched in the shoulders and turned in at the feet, and thus the beginning of a style was born. When one sees a number beginning with the dancers standing in a Turned-in Stance, the immediate thought is that it will most likely be a Fosse work.

To accomplish this stance, begin with the right foot turned in and the right leg straight. The weight should be shifted to the right, and this is seen in the right hip. The left leg is slightly bent, and the left foot is turned in. The arms may be in a variety of positions, but if they are down, they hang with the right shoulder lower than the left, which is raised. The image for the upper body is of a suit on a tilted hanger (figure 7.10; figure 7.11 shows a variation on the stance).

Figure 7.10

Figure 7.11

Rug Pull

Gwen Verdon referred to the following as a "Rug Pull." To get into it, rise to relevé, with knees bent and the upper body in a "hinge." Look back over a shoulder with the focus toward the ground. The arms are up. The wrists are flexed. There are variations on this. The entire look is to project that of a rug being pulled out from underneath you. The facial expression should be that of complete surprise (figure 7.12).

Figure 7.12

8

Steps

This section is going to concentrate on particular steps that, in some cases, use the information from the previous chapters as building blocks. One should master what has been explained previously before moving on to concentrate on the following movements.

Joe Frisco

For the purposes of this description, the arms will be straight in front of the body with hands flexed. The movement begins with the body facing SL, the right leg straight and the left leg in tendu toward SL (figure 8.1). The legs simply change positions repeatedly in Joe Frisco. The standing leg bends as it moves to the tendu position. At the end

Figure 8.1

Figure 8.2

the standing leg is always straight. A frequent error made by inexperienced dancers in this style is that they bend the standing leg. This should never happen. The torso and hips are neutral until one of the legs is in the tendu position, when the back is arched and the derrière is protruding in the back. As the switch is occurring, the torso undulates from the arched position to the neutral position. Once the legs stop, with the standing leg straight and the other leg in the tendu position, the torso is arched once again (figures 8.1 through 8.4). The counts are [and 1, and 2, etc.]. The tendu position with the back arched occurs on [1].

Figure 8.3

Figure 8.4

Gazelle Leaps

These require a running preparation after which you lift into the air with both legs bent and wide apart. If the right knee is up, the left arm is extended forward and is, ideally, curved downward, while the right arm is extended toward the back of the body and is also ideally curved downward. The focus is down toward the floor during the actual leap. As the leap occurs, the pathway should cut an arc in the air, with significant hang time at the peak (figures 8.5 through 8.7).

Figure 8.5

Figure 8.6

Figure 8.7

Messaround

This is an example of a movement that can easily be overdone. It should be executed very subtly. The arms can be held in a variety of ways; for the purpose of this example, they will be extended above the head with the wrists broken and the hands relaxed. The feet are in parallel first position and stay fairly close together. The legs are in a slight plié. The focus is down toward the floor near the right foot.

First, the feet: Push off with the ball of the right foot and step on the left. The

Figure 8.8

push-off occurs close to the left foot. This is repeated over and over again as you make a circle in place. Next, the hips: As the right ball pushes off, the hips circle from the left around to the right. As the hips complete the circle to the right, step on the left foot (figures 8.8 through 8.17). During the entire movement, the legs are slightly bent and the rotation of the body is in a counterclockwise direction. Overdoing it occurs when the hips are overextended. The counts are the push-off on [1], the hip circle on [2], the next push-off on [3], and the following hip circle on [4], and so on.

Figure 8.9

Figure 8.10

Figure 8.11

Figure 8.12

Figure 8.13

Figure 8.14

Figure 8.15

Figure 8.16

Figure 8.17

Slop Step

This can be done in a variety of ways. Here, we will concentrate on the step to the front and to the back.

The Slop Step to the front is a subtle step. The feet begin in parallel first. Step to the left foot. The leg should be slightly bent. As soon as the weight has transferred to that foot, allow the toes of the left foot to lift, rotate on the left heel until the left foot is turned out, and then lower the toes to the ground. When the step to the left foot is taken, the right heel lifts off the ground. Both legs are bent and the pelvis is tilted forward. The toes of the right foot drag through until they reach the front of the body and the weight is transferred (figures 8.18 and 8.19). The pelvis tilt and the foot drag occur simultaneously. The movement is completed once the toes of the standing foot hit the ground. The opposite foot then slides into position as the movement is repeated, alternating continuously. The step is on [1] and the toes lower on [2], and so on.

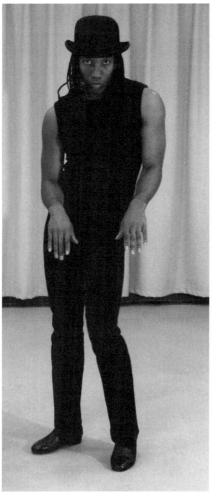
Figure 8.18

Figure 8.19

There are a variety of positions for the hands. In the pictures here, the arms are in New York Times position in front of the body. Note that the focus is tilted downward but the dancer is looking at the audience from under the brim of his derby. It should also be mentioned that if the step to the standing leg has a slight slide on the floor before it takes the weight, it is sometimes called "skating."

The other Slop Step to be described here is the one that the dancer does moving US while facing the audience. When doing this particular step, Fosse Arms are used. Step to the right foot on [1]. As this happens the left hip lifts and the outside portion of the left foot traces an arc from front to back. As the left foot is working, the arms are moving to the left. Both legs are in plié. As soon as the foot reaches the back while tracing the arc, the weight transfers to the left foot on [2] (figures 8.20 and 8.21).

The Slop Step alternates repeatedly. It should be done in a very loose and undulating manner.

Figure 8.20   Figure 8.21

Charlie Chaplin

This is a step that shows the whimsical side of Fosse. The step appears to be relatively easy, but the difficulty lies in moving the feet correctly. The movement is very small.

Standing in turned-out first position with the legs straight, arms down at the side, and hands touching the outside of the thighs, begin by stepping forward a couple of inches with the right heel, keeping the feet turned out. Allow the foot to roll to the ground after the heel hits. Next, bend the left leg slightly, step in front of the right foot, heel first, and put it down, heel first, and roll the left foot down. Repeat the two steps.

Now add the shoulders. As you step on the right foot, the right shoulder rolls up and backward; when the step is made to the left foot, the left shoulder rolls up and backward. The shoulder rolls are done as isolations.

As mentioned, the difficulty lies in the footwork. The steps are obvious, but "working the floor" with each foot is the challenge. Note that each step occurs on a count (figure 8.22).

Figure 8.22

Snake Hips

Begin with feet in parallel first position, knees bent, and torso bent over so that the focus is toward the floor and slightly in front of the feet. The weight shifts to the right foot on [and] as the left foot moves out to the left slightly on [1], legs still bent, feet still parallel, and toes of the left foot on the ground. The left foot returns to its starting position on the next [and], and the right foot moves to the right slightly, legs still bent, feet still parallel, and toes of the right foot on the ground on [2].

While the leg movement is going on, the arms are working independently. When the left foot is out, the left arm has floated and the right arm is down by the right side and softly bent. The arms change position to the same side as the foot that is out. Note that the arm movement is always initiated by the elbow, moves to the wrist, and then to the hand. Initially, the movement with the arms is not large, and they undulate fairly closely to the sides of the body.

Then slowly lift the torso and change the level of focus while the legs extend more and more with each sequence and the arms change level (figures 8.23 through 8.25).

Figure 8.23

Figure 8.24

Figure 8.25

Crescent Jumps

These are very exciting. The preparation is a plié in parallel first position, arms down and loose. Jump as high as possible, sending the body into an arc in the air with the curve of the arc facing SL. The left foot lifts in parallel up the inside right leg to the beginning of the calf muscle. The arms are straight and overhead with Splayed Fingers, and they follow the arc of the body to the left.

Note that the accompanying pictures show the landing and the subsequent step forward into fourth position, with turned-out right foot and heel of the left foot up. Both arms are softly bent as the left arm is lifted upward on the diagonal and the right arm is slightly behind the body on the same diagonal as the left. The body is angled toward the left DS corner, the hands are flexed, and the focus is up and toward the left hand. Note that the knees are together. This position ends a Crescent Jump so that it can be repeated (figures 8.26 through 8.28).

Figure 8.26

Figure 8.27

Figure 8.28

Shoeshine

This typifies the quirkiness and whimsy that people enjoy so much in Fosse's work. The movement is stationary. Begin with the left leg in plié and the foot slightly turned in. With the right leg in parallel, the upper portion of the right foot is turned in and "hooked" to the left leg around the back, below the back of the knee. The torso can be bent over or up, and the focus is either to the floor or slightly toward the audience.

The arms can vary. In figures 8.29 and 8.30, the right hand holds the brim of the derby with Teacup Fingers, and the left hand is on the hip with Splayed Fingers. The arms are also frequently down by the sides of the body and are straight. The wrists are flexed, and the palms of the hands face the floor. From either body position, the right leg moves up and down the calf of the left leg, giving the impression of shining the top of the right shoe by rubbing it against the left pant leg. While this is occurring, the body does not change level.

Figure 8.31 shows another version of Shoeshine. In a slight lunge on the left leg with the right leg extended, left hand on the hip, and left elbow pinned back, brush the back of the fingers of the right hand across the top of the right foot, again as if to shine the shoe. The focus is toward that foot. The arm movement begins with a soft right arm moving down and across the body until the fingertips brush across the top of the right foot. The arm then follows through in a softly bent position.

Figure 8.29

Figure 8.30

Figure 8.31

Charity March

This is named after a step executed in the musical *Sweet Charity*. In order to execute this step correctly, begin in turned-out first position with the left arm bent, the left hand in front of the stomach with palm facing in and Splayed Fingers, the right arm

Figure 8.32

Figure 8.33

bent with palm facing the audience, Splayed Fingers, and the forearm parallel to the plane of the floor. Step to the left foot, which is turned out, allow the weight to shift to the left hip, and bring the right foot up to a turned-out passé with a flexed foot. At the same time, the left shoulder Scissors downward and the right shoulder rises. Next, step to the right foot while the left moves to turned out passé with flexed foot. Each step is on a count.

The arms do not change position on the weight shift to the right foot; however, the shoulders do. The left shoulder rises, and the right shoulder scissors downward (figures 8.32 and 8.33).

Boogaloo

The boogaloo was a dance craze in the 1960s. Here, however, I use it to describe a movement Fosse created and made his own. The step feels very awkward to do when first attempted but soon can be effortless.

The legs are in parallel second position and are straight. The arms are above the head and are not parallel to each other but are angled outward with the palms of the hands facing downward, fingertips of one hand facing the fingertips of the other. The footwork is just small steps with straight legs, during which the hands flap out and in two times on counts [and 1, and 2]: step on the right leg, flap the hands out and in twice; step on the left leg, flap the hands out and in twice.

Add the hips. The derrière bumps back twice on the right step, and twice again on the left step. Add the head. The focus is down toward the working foot. On each step, the head bumps back twice.

The difficulty of this step is that so many parts of the body are moving in different directions. The breakdown is not pictured.

Pippin Bows

Different versions of these bows can be seen in the musical *Pippin*. Several Pippin Bow poses are illustrated in figure 8.34. A description of the actual movement into two of the poses is detailed here, but note that there are many ways to get into these poses.

For the first bow, done by Nicole (left), the legs are in second, turned-out position. Plié and keep the toes of the left foot on the ground as the right heel is raised. Begin with arms overhead and softly bent. Plié more deeply as the arms open and the wrists do Wrist Curls with neither extended fingers nor fists. Before the bow is completed, the Wrist Curls cease and hands open with the palms facing the audience and Splayed Fingers. The plié deepens and the fingers stay splayed until the bow is completed. The arms end up broken at the elbows. In this description, the left arm is higher than the right. This bow is also frequently done with the heel rather than the toes on the ground.

The second bow, executed by Noel (center), begins with the left foot turned out and the right in tendu toward the audience but with the heel rather than the toes on the floor. In other words, the audience sees the bottom of the foot. As the plié begins and deepens on the left leg, the arms, which are curved and overhead, start to open up to the side with Wrist Curls. The head bows slowly until the focus is to the ground. Note that the leg in tendu is also bent. Just prior to this, the wrists stop curling and the palms of the hands face the audience with Splayed Fingers. The arms are in Broken Doll position as the bow is being executed once the Wrist Curls have ceased.

Figure 8.34

Bedroom Slippers

The image for doing this particular movement is wearing backless bedroom slippers and shuffling along in them. The legs are in parallel first position in a slight plié. The step is executed in place or moving forward slightly. If it is done in place, the foot simply slides forward and back. If it is done with a move forward, the foot slides forward slightly and the heel, which is barely off the ground, lowers.

Add hips. As the foot slides forward, the pelvis moves forward; as the heel lowers to the ground, the pelvis moves back. Add Hip Cranks (described in chapter 1: Moves).

As the foot moves forward, the wrist is broken and the knuckles of the hand are facing the floor. As the foot lowers to the ground and the pelvis moves back, the heels of the hands push back and the knuckles face front (figures 8.35 through 8.39).

The foot slides forward on [1] and back to parallel first on [2], and so on.

Figure 8.35

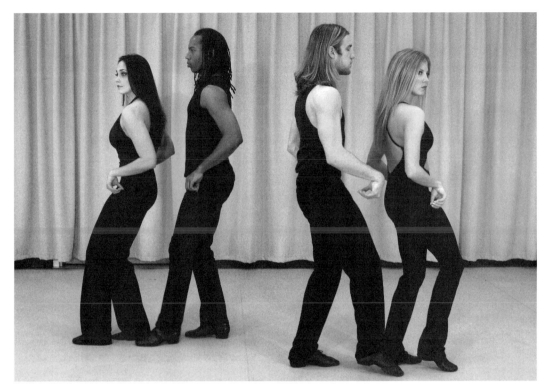

Figure 8.36

Figure 8.37

Figure 8.38

Figure 8.39

Monkey Down

Begin with the feet together and parallel, legs straight. The hands are in front of the chest, both in Soft-Boiled-Egg position. Monkey Hands will be used. Slowly lower into a grand plié, the hands precisely changing position so that the right is down and the left is up. Midway through each hand change, do a Head Knock: a fast movement of the head down and up. It barely moves downward (with the face still in the same orientation) before it rebounds back to the original position.

Note that the wrists do a very well defined break during this movement. The hands continue to change position during the plié. When the grand plié is completed, and the heels of the feet are off the ground, return slowly to standing position with the same arm work (figures 8.40 through 8.47). Note that each Head Knock and hand change occur on the same count.

Figure 8.40

Figure 8.41

Figure 8.42

Figure 8.43

Figure 8.44

Figure 8.45

Figure 8.46

Figure 8.47

Mechanical Boxer

This movement recalls the toy robotic boxers from the 1960s. Two dancers are needed to do it. The woman should be in a "closed," wide, turned-in fourth position with the back heel up, and the man should directly face her in an open, turned-in fourth position with the back heel up. They should be close enough so that when their torsos are bent over, their foreheads touch. Their legs will overlap. The men's arm positions pictured are DS hand fisted low and arm forward with the elbow prominently bent, and the US hand fisted, arm broken at the elbow and raised significantly back.

With fists almost touching, the partners move their arms forward and back smoothly as if they are punching each other on counts [1, 2, 3]. On [4], they do a slight contraction in the pelvis. The sequence then continues.

Note that in figure 8.48 the dancers are seen in the punch position, while in figure 8.49 they have landed the third punch and are in a contraction.

Figure 8.48

Figure 8.49

Rocking Horse

This move uses Saucer Hands. The legs are open wide during the movement. The weight of the dancer shifts heavily back to the left leg on counts [1, 2], and as that happens, the leg goes into a plié as the right leg rises in a turned-out attitude forward with toes pointed. The weight then shifts smoothly to the right leg, which sinks into plié as the torso tips forward slightly and the left leg rises in a turned-out attitude on counts [3, 4].

Note that the torso faces the audience, the head is slightly tilted and remains that way, and the legs are in an open position. When this movement is done continuously, smoothly, and properly, it looks like a rocking horse (figures 8.50 and 8.51).

Figure 8.50

Figure 8.51

Pecking Chug

For this, the motion of Hip Cranks is done continuously, but the hands are not flush against the sides of the hips. The head does a peck to the front as the heel of the hand pushes back, and then moves back as soon as the hand begins cranking again.

This is a traveling step used to move all around the stage. To accomplish this (and for the purposes of description), step to the left foot on [1]. As soon as it receives the weight, it chugs forward and the right foot drags in parallel so that its toes are against the area right above the left ankle on [2]. The chug takes place as the Hip Crank is occurring. Once the chug ends but before you step to the right foot in order to repeat the entire movement, the heels of the hands are pushed back, and at the end of the cranking the head is isolated and pushed forward. Repeat all continuously (figures 8.52 through 8.54).

Figure 8.52

Figure 8.53

Figure 8.54

Step Together with Back Bumps

This title is almost self-explanatory. For the purpose of this description, face SL, with the right side of the body toward the audience. The right arm is extended, the right wrist is flexed, and the palm of the hand is facing the audience. The hand is just below the face so that the face is not covered. The left elbow is up and the left hand is holding the brim of the derby with Teacup Fingers. The footwork is simply stepping DS

Figure 8.55

with the right foot and then bringing the left foot to the right foot, done in parallel plié.

Add the movement with the derrière. As the right foot steps DS, the derrière bumps backward two times [1, 2]. As the left foot moves to join the right foot in parallel first position, the derrière once again executes two bumps backward [3, 4]. Note that these bumps are done lightly and without force (figures 8.55 through 8.58).

Figure 8.56

Figure 8.57

Figure 8.58

Crossed Leg with Isolations

Begin in turned-out first position with both legs straight. The right leg does a battement with a flexed foot to second position. Then the knee bends and the area above the right ankle rests on the thigh just above the left knee. As the right leg bends, the left leg lowers into plié.

As the right leg does the battement, the arms open into a straight-armed second position, the palms facing the audience with Splayed Fingers. The arms hold until the full leg movement is completed. Then take the thumb and forefinger of the hands and move them to the area in front of the pelvic bone, with the remainder of the fingers softly extended, slightly curled, and backs of the hands facing each other. The wrists are broken. Turn the hands over, keeping the shape, so that the palms face the audience. Bring the left fist to the left hipbone and the right arm back to its opening position but with the hand in a fist.

Finally, the right hand fisted does Wrist Curls, the hips do a Hip Circle counterclockwise, and the right ankle circles. All of the circles occur simultaneously on two counts (figures 8.59 through 8.65).

Figure 8.59

Figure 8.60

Figure 8.61

Figure 8.62

Figure 8.63

Figure 8.64

Figure 8.65

Bourrées with Hip Circles

This is another step that can be done in a variety of ways. For the purpose of this explanation, the hands will be in Saucer position.

Start in first position parallel, in relevé but with a plié. As the bourrées commence, the hips whip quickly in a circle, clockwise to the left on the count of [1] and then circle around to the back, to the right, and to neutral on [2, 3, 4]. The movement is done continuously so that the Hip Circles never stop (figures 8.66 through 8.69).

Figure 8.66

Figure 8.67

Figure 8.68

Figure 8.69

Shim Sham with Shimmy and East Indian Hands

Begin in parallel first position. The arms and hands are in the East Indian position. Plié and then send the right heel out in front of the body with a slight bend in the knee, the heel hitting the ground on [1]. The right foot immediately comes back to parallel first on [2]. Repeat with the left foot [3, 4]. Next, the right foot repeats shooting forward and hitting the heel on [5], but when it returns to parallel, the ball of the foot touches on [6]. There is no weight change, and the right foot repeats the motion on [7]. When the right foot returns on [8], put the weight on both feet so that the movement can be repeated on the other side. Throughout the entire movement the shoulders shimmy as quickly as possible (figures 8.70 through 8.74).

Figure 8.70

Figure 8.71

Figure 8.72

Figure 8.73

Figure 8.74

Cannonballs

Begin with a running preparation into a parallel first plié. Then bring the knees together up in the air and do a flick kick with the DS leg as the US leg moves toward the floor. Both arms are stretched forward parallel as the flick kick occurs.

Once the kick has been accomplished and the US foot is on the floor with the leg bent, the DS leg comes to parallel passé, and the arms circle down and fling back behind the head, as the back bends and the head is thrown back (figures 8.75 through 9.87). Recover, take two steps, and repeat the movement.

This entire step, from the standing preparation to the final back arch, is done in three counts. The preparation for the actual jump is on [1], the hang time in the air is on [2], and the final pose is hit on [3]. The arch is held for an additional count [4]. The next two preparation steps occur on [5, 6] and [7, 8]. This movement requires a great amount of strength and flexibility. When done well, it is a showstopper.

Figure 8.75

Figure 8.76

Figure 8.77

Figure 8.78

Figure 8.79

Figure 8.80

Figure 8.81

Figure 8.82

Figure 8.83

Figure 8.84

Figure 8.85

Figure 8.86

Figure 8.87

Knuckle Knocks

This is an extremely offbeat but beautiful movement. Begin with the weight on the right leg, which is straight. The left foot is raised to the ball or toes and is several inches forward of the right foot. The body is pulled up out of the hips, which creates a long, lean look. The body is very slightly angled toward the left. The derrière does four light Back Bumps with the body in this position on [1, 2, 3, 4]. The elbows are close to the body but not pinned to the sides, the wrists break, and the fingers bend at the knuckles and lightly touch the top of each palm. The thumbs are held in.

Now the heels of the hands tap the sides of the hips at hipbone level twice, at the same time as the first two Back Bumps with the hips. The hands move up to the waist, elbows opening up, and the knuckles tap the waist once on the third Back Bump. The palm should be facing up. The hands then move up the body to the sides of the chest, at breast level, with elbows close to the body, and the heels of the hands tap once on the fourth Back Bump. Shift the weight to the left foot and reverse the entire movement on [5, 6, 7, 8].

Once it is completed, the body shifts back to the original position, angled slightly to the left, and both arms rise above the head: elbows, wrists, hands in succession. As the arms move overhead and end with the wrists broken, the derrière does four Back Bumps on [1, 2, 3, 4]. Both feet rise to the balls and the feet pivot so that the body swivels to angle toward the SR diagonal on [5], and then swivels again to angle toward the SL diagonal on [6]. There is one more swivel toward the SR diagonal on [7], and then the left heel lowers to the ground, the right heel stays popped as both legs sink into a plié. As this is happening, the derrière does two quick Back Bumps on [and 8] and the arms gently lower: elbows, wrists, and hands in succession. The entire sequence is done in two sets of eight counts (figures 8.88 through 8.101).

Figure 8.88

Figure 8.89

Figure 8.90

Figure 8.91

Figure 8.94

Figure 8.92

Figure 8.93

Figure 8.95

Figure 8.96

Figure 8.97

Figure 8.100

Figure 8.98

Figure 8.99

Figure 8.101

Mambo Combination

Gwen Verdon spent many hours at Broadway Theatre Project describing the various segments that together create this movement. Listening to her extensive explanations and analogies was a privilege for all of us. In particular, she wanted us to understand how to execute an unorthodox movement while still maintaining the correct balance, working with a hat, and moving into a direction change.

To begin, step DS on the left foot, holding a hat to the chest with both hands on [1]. The dome of the hat is facing the audience. The right foot then steps to the right, and both legs move into a low parallel plié as the hips Dust the Piano Bench from right to left and the weight shifts from right to left on [2]. At the same time, the right hand takes the hat and with a "soft" right arm moves it in a circle from the right of the body to the front of the body, where it is again held against the chest by two hands. Gwen Verdon referred to this arm movement as Scooping Sugar. The left hand is in a fist on the left hip.

Next, step DS on the right foot on [3], and lift the left leg into a parallel passé with a flexed foot. Note that the leg creates a right angle, as the foot is not actually touching the knee. As the left leg rises, the right foot chugs and the shoulders do a very quick shimmy, all on [4].

Step on the left foot DS on [5], do a fast Hook or low rond de jambe with the right foot, which turns the body to face SL, and end in a wide, open, turned-in fourth position with the right heel popped on [6].

Finally, do two heel drops with the right foot on [7, 8]. As the heel hits the ground,

Figure 8.102

the arms shoot out in front of the body with the hat in both hands, and as the heel rises off the ground, the arms bend and come back to the chest. This sequence is done twice. The entire movement is done in eight counts (figures 8.102 through 8.112).

Figure 8.103

Figure 8.104

Figure 8.105

Figure 8.107

Figure 8.106

Figure 8.108

Figure 8.109

Figure 8.111

Figure 8.110

Figure 8.112

Bourrées with Port du Bras

To begin, the feet are in first position parallel with the legs slightly bent. To do the bourrées, the weight shifts to the right hip and the feet move to the right. The weight then shifts to the left hip and the feet move to the left.

Add the arms. Moving to the right, lift the right arm into an arch with the inside of the elbow facing the side of the body and the left arm dropped into an arch with the inside of the elbow facing the ceiling. Both arms move first with the elbows, then the wrists, and finally the hands. Repeat to the left, the arms reversing their actions (figures 8.113 through 8.116, the movement without the bourrées; figures 8.117 and 8.118, with the foot movement added).

Figure 8.113

Figure 8.114

Figure 8.115

Figure 8.116

Figure 8.117

Figure 8.118

Electric Shocks

This is an exciting sequence, made all the more so because it involves a considerable amount of improvisation. Basically, the body, arms, and head are thrown out or up with reckless abandon, as if you have been electrically "shocked." After the shock happens on [1], a "melting" occurs on [2, 3, 4]. The melting is almost as if the body is deflating (see figures 8.119 through 8.125 for one example).

Figure 8.119

Figure 8.120

Figure 8.122

Figure 8.121

Figure 8.123

Figure 8.124

Figure 8.125

Throwing Wet Tissue

This pertains to giving a slight toss of the hand from the wrist, as if attempting to dislodge a piece of wet tissue paper from the fingers. It is an easy concept to grasp. Note that this movement involves only the wrist and the hand (figures 8.126 through 8.128).

Figure 8.126

Figure 8.127

Figure 8.128

Front Hat Trick

Fosse was fond of hat tricks. This is an example of one of them. Begin facing the audience in an open fourth position, turned in, with the right foot forward and the left foot back. The left heel is popped. The right hand holds the side of the derby by the brim at waist level, and the left hand is straight up from the left shoulder with the left wrist broken in preparation to catch the hat. (Figure 8.129) Lightly toss the hat upward without moving the right hand to a great degree. As the hat travels upward, it revolves once (figure 8.130). Then catch the US side of the brim, so that the dome of the derby is toward the ceiling (figure 8.131).

Figure 8.129

Figure 8.130

Figure 8.131

Grand Battement with Layout

To execute this very difficult movement, step to the left foot on relevé and do a battement with the right leg. Note that the right arm is moving to the right diagonal and the left arm is moving upward (figure 8.132). As the battement rises, begin to release in the back as the legs continue extending (figure 8.133). Finally, completely release in the back and the head. At this point, the right arm is extended back on a diagonal and the left arm is extended upward (figure 8.134). This is, perhaps, one of the most beautiful of Fosse's moves.

Figure 8.132

Figure 8.133

Figure 8.134

9

Facial Expression

While auditioning dancers for *Chicago*, I knew it was important that I convey to them the facial expression needed to draw the audience in at the top of the show. I told the dancers to focus their eyes over the tops of the heads of the audience members as if they were boring a hole through the back wall. This was referred to as Bullet Eyes, an analogy that is very useful in several numbers Fosse choreographed. The look generates a sense of mystery for the audience. It is important for the faces of the dancers to be interesting and inviting in a subtle way (figure 9.1). Note, however, that for many

Figure 9.1

numbers, a smile is the perfect facial expression. The point here is that the face is important in conveying a message to the audience. Dancing does not just involve the body.

Note that in figure 9.2, the dancers are in a group but are, in essence, not in a group. They are positioned close together, but if one looks at their faces, it is evident that each displays a different thought going on and that they are focusing in many directions. The looks on the faces are enticing and make the audience want to know more about each member of that group.

Figure 9.2

10

Group Movement

Clump

This is simply a group of dancers placed very close together so that they touch each other. The movements described here are formed by what the dancers do with their bodies once they are in a Clump.

Amoeba

This is one of the most popular images in the Fosse style. It requires a group of dancers. The more there are, the more interesting shapes there are to be created and the more stories to be told. The idea is to have the dancers in a tight Clump, so close that they are touching. It can be stationary or move across the floor.

Figure 10.1

Once the Clump has been created, the dancers improvise, using each other to create different silhouettes and group images. They are constantly moving arms, legs, torsos, hips, and focus. They create their own internal stories, and a world of information is on the stage for just a moment.

Figure 10.2

Figure 10.3

Figure 10.6

Figure 10.7

The four dancers pictured have created a very small Amoeba, but as one moves through the sequence, the shapes and stories are still evident (figures 10.1 through 10.9). Note that in these pictures, the Amoeba is stationary.

Figure 10.4

Figure 10.5

Figure 10.8

Figure 10.9

Can of Worms

This is an Amoeba, but it concentrates on the arms working in all directions and levels. The torso, legs, feet, and hips can obviously help to create more interesting shapes, so that the arm movements are more intricate and more effective. This is usually a stationary group movement.

Seaweed

This movement first involves the formation of a Clump. It is reliant upon the arms, just as Can of Worms is, but here the arms are waving and undulating in the same direction, just like seaweed behaves underwater, moving in the direction of the current. The torso and hips are involved here. Occasionally, one might see an "errant" strand or two of this seaweed moving against the current for the sake of an interesting twist.

Stack

A Fosse Stack can be identified almost immediately. In the discussion here, the focus is on the arms.

To create this picture, several dancers stand in a vertical line facing US, so that the audience essentially sees only the DS dancer; the other dancers are not as visible. One example of a Stack has the DS dancer raise the hands and slightly flare them away from the hips. As the observer's eye travels US, it sees that each dancer has arms raised a little higher. The dancer farthest US has arms overhead. The image is that of a many-armed figure. It is very likely that other parts of the body are involved in order to make the entire picture more interesting, such as the breaking of the wrist and a snapping of the fingers. There are many other variations of a Stack (figure 10.10).

Figure 10.10

11

The Dancer as Actor

This section has been added because Fosse believed vehemently that his dancers should not just be dancers but must also be actors. This needs explanation because most dancers are taught the fundamentals of ballet, tap, and jazz, which alone are a plateful. Currently, many dancers are trained in pyrotechnics and are moving from one competition to another. Whether a dancer is interested in pursuing musical theatre or dance as a career or wishes to continue competing, the one who has an understanding of acting and can implement it when moving is a deeper performer who brings more meaning to the choreography. Note in figure 11.1 that the dancer is conveying by his movement and facial expression that he is conjuring up some sort of magic.

Figure 11.1

Think of a layering process when readying a piece for performance. The first thing that comes into play is the years of technique that have gone into making this dancer a technician. After years of this education, the choreography must be placed on the dancer, and the execution of that choreography must be accomplished at a high level. Some dancers stop after this has been done. There is one layer remaining, however, that is crucial in making a good dancer a great dancer, and that is acting.

As has been shown numerous times in this book, Fosse had an image for almost every step. This image was something for the dancers to focus on, and only thumbnail sketches have been offered here. If one looks at Fosse's complete body of work,

Figure 11.2

Figure 11.3

Figure 11.4

Figure 11.5

Figure 11.6

Figure 11.7

from the beginning of each number to the end, it becomes amply clear that each number is filled with imagery and, in some cases, one image guides the entire number. In figures 11.2 through 11.5, Zane pushes his hair back and stares into a mirror. The intensity of his expression makes you interested in what is going on in his mind. In figure 11.6, he also appears to be staring into a mirror, but his expression is very different, yet just as interesting. In figure 11.7, Noel is on the floor, one arm reaching farther than the other. He has flipped his head up in order to look at the audience. The expression on his face and the obvious tension in his body make this deeper than just movement.

Continuing with examples, figures 11.8 through 11.12 are associated with the number "Rich Man's Frug." (There are three parts to this number, but here only the first two are discussed.) The first part is called "The Aloof" and is an example of an exclusive set of people who are extremely wealthy and have a definite sense of entitlement. Ms. Verdon instructed the men to raise an eyebrow or flare a nostril in order to get across to the audience that they have little regard for those other than in their own set. The second part of this number is "The Heavyweight." Verdon explained that Fosse was an avid fan of the boxer "Sugar" Ray Robinson and that is why he was interested in going in this direction in the piece. So a boxing motif defines this part; one can still see the exclusivity in the dancers' faces, but they are beginning to "loosen up" at this party, competing a little and flirting a little.

Figure 11.8

Figure 11.10

Figure 11.11

Figure 11.9

Figure 11.12

"Big Spender" is a very important acting piece. I mention this because Gwen Verdon spent much time speaking about the character each woman was to convey. This is a dance hall, and the characters are desperate for the next dance in order to make money. The dancers make up their own stories in order to motivate their actions throughout the number. Thus the room is filled with many women with just as many different personalities (figure 11.13). One wonderful image that Ms. Verdon gave the dancers is that even though they are drooping from fatigue on the bar, their ankles "broken" and feet rolled over from a very long night of dancing, there is the sense of a sewing-machine needle moving rapidly within their stomachs, reminding them that they must bring money home in order to live. There is an urgency that these ladies must feel, although it is never telegraphed by the body. The face gives the observer a hint of what each character is like.

Figure 11.13

Figure 11.14 clearly shows a good-looking man flirting with a good-looking woman. The connection between the two dancers is obvious. In figure 11.15 the central character is clearly flirting with the young lady behind him as the one in front checks over her shoulder to see what is happening. She is watching and waiting for the moment the attention goes to her.

Figure 11.14

Figure 11.15

"Cool Hand Luke" is one of the most beautiful numbers choreographed by Fosse, probably because it is the first number he choreographed for his wife, Ms. Verdon, after the birth of their child, Nicole. Verdon spent much time with the dancers explaining the image of a bandit riding in rough terrain. She explained that during certain moments, one can see the bandit, while at others the horse is the focus. The Bandit pose has been seen earlier. In figures 11.16 and 11.17 the image is that of a horse prancing on a rocky path. The focus is down as the animal watches for snakes in its path.

Figure 11.16

Figure 11.17

Note in figure 11.18, the dancers move into a low attitude in relevé, but their focus is back and toward the ground. Here the image is that the horse has seen the snake and is stepping over it. In figure 11.19, however, the horse is spooked, rearing up, and one soon sees the dancers fall to their knees. Hearing Ms. Verdon explain the analogies for this number was both enlightening and a privilege.

Figure 11.18

Figure 11.19

Figure 11.20 shows a "flight crew" welcoming people on board. The young woman on the ground closest to SR is pointing to the crew and introducing them. They certainly do not look like one's usual flight attendants. In figure 11.21, two men are vying for the attention of one beautiful woman. She wants both and has, in fact, chosen them. She eventually exits with both men.

Figure 11.20

Figure 11.21

In figure 11.22, one can see upon inspection that the dancers are "seeing" something happening. They have slightly different expressions on their faces, but it is clear that something has drawn their attention.

A blank-faced dancer or one who has a "stage smile" pasted on the face and nothing going on behind the eyes is a dancer who is often left behind during auditions. Overemoting is not acceptable, either. Besides being well trained, a dancer will give a riveting performance by thinking about the music and the movement beforehand and trying to attach meaning to it. If one thinks of Fosse's dancers—Ben Vereen, Gwen Verdon, Chita Rivera, Ann Reinking, Liza Minnelli, Shirley MacLaine, and the myriad other extraordinary dancers who passed through his shows—it is clear that each and every one possessed something different, something magical that accompanied beautiful dance technique. This was no accident. They looked alive, they understood the reason they were doing each step, and were able to execute the steps with finesse and beauty. Never underestimate the worth of a "thinking" dancer who takes time to do homework on the choreography, the impetus behind the movement, and the music.

Figure 11.22

12

Choreography
by Debra McWaters
in the Fosse Style

My choreography for this section uses the vocabulary detailed in the previous chapters. The pictures in this chapter are taken from earlier chapters and should serve as an aid in executing the choreography. Note that in many cases, what is asked of the dancer by the choreography might not be exactly what is seen in the picture. There will be a strong relationship, however. In several cases, certain movements and poses are left to the dancer to create and execute, but it is to be done in the Fosse style.

Music selected for this combination should be in 4/4 time with a sixteenth note and rock-gospel feel. It should also have 112 beats per minute.

The dancer begins by facing the audience. The legs are together, the feet are in parallel first position, and the hands are at the hipbones with Splayed Fingers (figure 12.1).

For the first eight counts, the dancer should very slowly begin to move. This is done in an improvisatory manner, but the result must be the pose explained below. The movement should be executed as if moving underwater or "oozing." The important thing to remember is that one must remain within the Fosse framework. This movement continues into the second eight counts until the dancer has settled into a Fosse pose by [6] of the second eight. Then [7, 8] should be held. Several examples of poses are exhibited here (figures 12.2 through 12.6). These are not the only poses allowed, however. The dancer can always create variations of what has been illustrated in previous chapters but must not deviate from the Fosse style.

The third and fourth eights are also improvisational, only the dancer must select a different pose to end at [6] of the fourth eight. Again, refer to the figures in the previous paragraph and other photographs in this book.

It is important to stop here and talk about improvising. There is great freedom in improvising, and it is a luxury when a dancer has the opportunity to create within a

Figure 12.1

Figure 12.2

Figure 12.3

Figure 12.4   Figure 12.5

piece. The common problem, however, is to rush the movement. That is why the terms *moving underwater*, *oozing*, and *taffy pull* are used to guide the dancer in the pacing and the basic "feel" of the slow improvisation used here. It is also true that there are times when improvisation is used within a number and the idea is not to move in this slow manner. Note that improvisation in this piece is not presentational. What is desired is an "internal and personal" feeling.

For the fifth and sixth eights, the idea continues. The dancer improvises completely for the full fifth eight and a third pose by [6] of the sixth eight. The same is done for the seventh and eighth eights. The goal is to hit a fourth pose by [6] of the eighth eight. Make an attempt to change the improvisation from one section to another. A good practice tool for becoming comfortable with improvising and also being brave enough to step out of the "box" and take chances with different movements is to put on music and improvise in front of the mirror. Once you become comfortable with this, it is sheer joy to dance.

The ninth eight begins with the right foot. Four Slop Steps, right, left, right, left, are done moving DS. There should be two counts per step. The arms should be in New York Times position (figure 12.7)

Figure 12.6

Figure 12.7

On the tenth eight, since the weight is on the left foot, the dancer does a pas de bourrée while turning to the right on [1 and 2]. The right foot should step behind the left in order to begin the pas de bourrée. Once the dancer is facing the audience again, a soutenu is done by crossing the left foot over the right and stepping to the right once the body faces the audience again on [3, 4]. Note that both the pas de bourrée and the soutenu should be done in a plié. Two more Slop Steps moving DS begin with the left foot on [5, 6], [7, 8].

For the eleventh eight, the dancer should execute two slow chaînés to the left in a small circle ending up facing the audience on [1, 2, 3, 4]. The weight ends on the right foot. For [5, 6, 7, 8] the dancer steps to the left foot and begins executing four quick Slop Steps moving US (figures 12.8 and 12.9)

The twelfth eight begins with pas de bourrée turning to the left with the left foot placed behind the right on [1 and 2]. Again, a soutenu occurs by placing the right foot in front of the left on [3, 4]. Now, the dancer moves DS doing Broken Doll with Shoulder Scissoring. The right foot steps forward first. The first two of these are done on [5, 6] (figure 12.10). On [7] continue with the movement but place the right foot forward, and on [8] pivot to face US. During [7] and [8], never drop the form. During Broken Doll, use Bullet Eyes (figures 12.11, 12.12, and 12.13).

Figure 12.8

Figure 12.9

Figure 12.10

Figure 12.11

Figure 12.12

Figure 12.13

Move US doing the Fosse Walk beginning with the right foot and with Soft-Boiled-Egg hands (figure 12.14). There are four steps, and each takes two counts. At the end of this, the thirteenth eight has just been completed. For the fourteenth eight, do two more Fosse Walks, two counts each, then stop on [5], pull the feet together in parallel position while the legs are in plié and continue doing four sets of Fosse Arms with hips engaged for [5, 6, 7, 8] (figures 12.15 and 12.16).

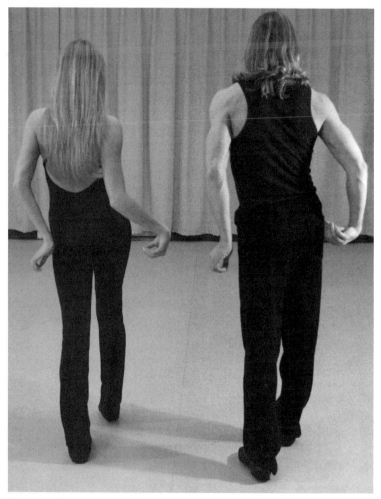

Figure 12.14

Figure 12.15

Figure 12.16

For the fifteenth eight, turn right quickly to face SL and take eight counts to Crank the right hip. The feet do not move. Each Crank takes two counts (figures 12.17 and 12.18). Note that for the last four counts of this eight, the dancer should look at the audience. The head moves slowly in order to do this. In other words, the head does a slow "cruise" to the audience. The expression is not a smile but is "knowing."

The sixteenth eight has the dancer doing a double turn to the right, with the left leg in parallel passé, both legs in plié, the body contracted over, the focus down, and the arms hugging the waist on [1, 2]. On [3], the left foot comes down to parallel first with legs together and body facing DS, the body straightens, and the arms toss up into the air in parallel and with a flick of the fingertips as if tossing tissue paper. The focus is upward. Collapse over on [4] with hands hugging shoulders, body contracted, and focus down. Raise the head slowly on [5, 6] and drum the fingers on each shoulder, beginning with the pinkie first and then moving sequentially through the other fingers, two times [7, 8]. Bullet Eyes should be employed here once the focus returns to the audience.

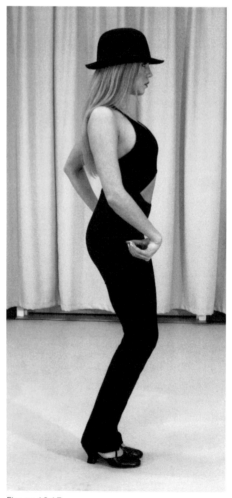 

Figure 12.17   Figure 12.18

The seventeenth eight through the twentieth eight are devoted to the port de bras outlined in detail in chapter 2 (figures 12.19 through 12.37). Each arm movement takes eight counts to be completed.

Figure 12.19

Figure 12.20

Figure 12.21

Figure 12.22

Figure 12.25

Figure 12.26

Figure 12.23

Figure 12.24

Figure 12.27

Figure 12.28

Figure 12.31

Figure 12.32

Figure 12.29

Figure 12.30

Figure 12.33

Figure 12.34

Figure 12.35

Figure 12.36

Figure 12.37

Now we will revisit improvising and pair it with the dancer's use of arms. This will comprise the twenty-first eight through the twenty-fourth eight. After completing the port de bras, eight counts are used to improvise slowly into a pose using New York Times Arms. The pose should occur on [7] of that eight. The same idea is used for the twenty-second eight, ending in a change of pose but still using New York Times Arms (figure 12.38). Repeat all of the above, but this time the poses should employ Drop of Water arms. This will occur twice, on the twenty-third eight and the twenty-fourth eight. Some examples of poses are in figures 12.39 and 12.40.

Figure 12.38

Figure 12.39

Figure 12.40

The twenty-fifth eight is devoted to the Messaround. Begin with the ball of the right foot for the push-off and circle to the left. The arms should reach toward the ceiling loosely and with the hands open and relaxed. The focus should be down toward

Figure 12.41

Figure 12.42

Figure 12.45

Figure 12.46

the right foot. The Hip Circles take two counts each: [1, 2], [3, 4], [5, 6], [7, 8] (figures 12.41 through 12.50). The dancer's weight is now on the left foot, and a complete circle with the body has been completed during the Messaround.

Figure 12.43

Figure 12.44

Figure 12.47

Figure 12.48

Figure 12.49

Figure 12.50

For the twenty-sixth eight, the dancer will do the Hip Roll Walk. The first step is to the ball of the right foot, and the right hip executes a tight clockwise circle. The arms are curved and behind the back. There should be no tension in the hands (figures 12.51 through 12.53). Each step takes two counts. The path of the walk is a curve to the right toward USR. The last step ends USC, and the right side of the dancer's body faces the audience.

Figure 12.51

Figure 12.52

Figure 12.53

Moving to the twenty-seventh eight, it can be seen that the weight is now on the left foot. The next movement is Step Together with Back Bumps. Each step takes two counts (figures 12.54 through 12.57)

Figure 12.54

Figure 12.55

Figure 12.56

Figure 12.57

The twenty-eighth eight involves four counts of the Messaround, moving once again in a circle around oneself to the left with the right foot initiating the movement. The rest of the movement is exactly as described above. At the end of the four counts, the dancer should be facing US. For [5, 6], the step is a "squish down" to the left in order to face the audience. This is simply a slow and oozy plié. The dancer can improvise on this. The [7, 8] requires the dancer to ease into a Fred Astaire position (figures 12.58 through 12.61)

Figure 12.58

Figure 12.59

Figure 12.60

Figure 12.61

The twenty-ninth eight through the thirtieth eight require the dancer to do the Knuckle Knocks. This is also repeated for the thirty-first eight through the thirty-second eight (figures 12.62 through 12.75)

Figure 12.62

Figure 12.63

Figure 12.64

Figure 12.65

Figure 12.66

Figure 12.67

Figure 12.70

Figure 12.71

Figure 12.68

Figure 12.69

Figure 12.72

Figure 12.73

Figure 12.74

Figure 12.75

The weight is now on the left foot. For the thirty-third eight, the dancer should do Snake Hips. The first foot to shoot out to the side should be the left foot on [1], after the right foot has taken a step on [and]. The right and left arms undulate to the left first. The undulation is very close to the body. The legs move out to the side very slightly. For the first four counts, the dancer should have the focus toward the floor and should be bent over slightly at the waist. The dancer raises the torso, the legs shoot out more, and the arms are higher in their undulation for the next four counts. The focus is now to the audience (figures 12.76 through 12.78).

Figure 12.76

Figure 12.77

Figure 12.78

The thirty-fourth eight finds the dancer now doing Bourrées with Port de Bras. The body is upright, the focus is to the audience with a slight smile on the face, the knees are bent, the legs are together and in plié, and the feet are parallel. The arms will be doing the same as described in chapter 8. The bourrées begin to the left on [1, 2], shift to the right on [3, 4], and so on until eight counts have been completed (figures 12.79 through 12.84)

Figure 12.79

Figure 12.80

Figure 12.81

Figure 12.83

Figure 12.82

Figure 12.84

The next step is Broken Doll in a wide circle to the left, with the left foot starting the movement and the shoulders scissoring (figures 12.85 and 12.86). There is only one eight in which to accomplish this—the thirty-fifth eight. Two counts should be allotted for each step. The dancer should end facing the audience.

Figure 12.85

Figure 12.86

Xs and Os occur for four counts on the thirty-sixth eight. The dancer moves toward SR and the preparation into loose fifth with the left foot in front should occur on the [and] before the [1] of the first eight (figures 12.87 and 12.88). After four counts, the dancer should improvise into a Hieroglyphic position of choice (figures 12.89 through 12.92).

Figure 12.87

Figure 12.88

Figure 12.89

Figure 12.91

Figure 12.90

Figure 12.92

213

On the thirty-seventh eight, the dancer should immediately face US, if not already doing so, and execute four Sable Brush Walks. Each step should take two counts. The right foot takes the first step (figures 12.93 and 12.94).

Figure 12.93

Figure 12.94

The dancer should face SR and with arms curved behind the back do four slow Leg Switches. The left leg should bend first. The focus should be toward the audience. A very slight smile would be appropriate. Each switch takes two counts. This will happen on the thirty-eighth eight (figure 12.95).

Figure 12.95

Both styles of Shoeshine are going to be danced for the thirty-ninth eight. First, step on the right foot and face the audience to execute the second version of Shoeshine, described in chapter 8 (figure 12.96). Four counts will be used for this version. It occurs first on the left foot for two counts and then on the right foot for two counts. For the remaining four counts, the dancer should Hook the right foot behind the left, and with arms down by the side and hands flexed, do two Shoeshines (figures 12.97 and 12.98).

Figure 12.96

Figure 12.97

Figure 12.98

The fortieth eight begins with the dancer putting the right foot down in parallel by the left foot with the legs together and in plié on [and] before [1]. Two slow Hip Swings should occur with hands on the hipbones and Splayed Fingers. The counts for these Hip Swings are [1, 2], [3, 4]. The first Hip Swing should be to the right. Complete the eight count by doing four fast and alternating Hip Swings with Saucer Hands. Each Hip Swing will take one count (figures 12.99 and 12.100).

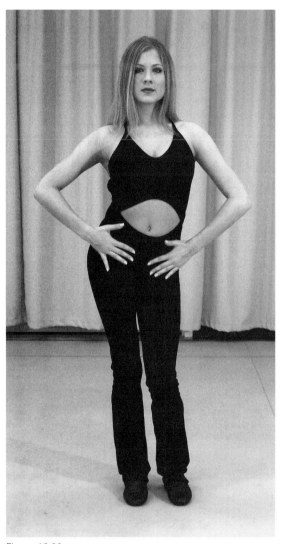

Figure 12.99

Figure 12.100

For the forty-first eight, rond de jambe the right leg with a flexed foot, in the air, from the back to the front and execute Crossed Leg with Isolations. The hands are in East Indian position (not pictured here). The right foot should make it to the left thigh on [8]. Keep the same position for the forty-second eight and isolate the hips so that they move in a very tight circle to the left. There should be four circles taking two counts each (figure 12.101).

Figure 12.101

The movement for the forty-third eight is a rond de jambe with the right foot, as described in the previous paragraph, only to the back so that it can Hook behind the left calf (figure 12.102). The hands should be in the Birdie Wing position (not pictured here). The forty-fourth eight is tight Hip Circles in this position. There should be three slow ones to the left on two counts to each, and then two fast ones for one count each.

Figure 12.102

For the forty-fifth eight through the forty-seventh eight, the dancer should slowly improvise in a taffy-pulling, oozy manner.

On the forty-eighth eight, the dancer slowly moves into the position seen in figure 12.103. The position should be reached by [6] with the head down. On [7, 8] the head slowly raises to look at the audience.

Figure 12.103

This completes the choreography using much of the Fosse movement as described in this book. Note that when choreographing a piece in the Fosse style, it is perfectly fine to use steps not pictured as long as they stay within the framework described here. I purposely did not use much connective tissue outside of what you have been reading in this book. This was done for learning purposes only.

Congratulations on learning a new dance style. Your assignments now should be to become comfortable with the information you have ingested and to watch as many movies containing the choreography of Bob Fosse as possible. There is much to learn and rehearse. Now you possess many explanations of this style, and you will be able to add to your visual palette by observing the style in action.

Index

Pages in *italics* indicate photographs.

Debra McWaters is a choreographer and the artistic director of the Broadway Theatre Project held at the University of South Florida each summer. She worked as Ann Reinking's associate for fifteen years. Together, they worked on Broadway shows such as *Chicago* and *Fosse*. Debra was the director-choreographer of the international tour of *Fosse* starring Ben Vereen. She has choreographed Ben Vereen's one-man show saluting Sammy Davis Jr. and is teaching master classes around the country. She recently workshopped a new Broadway musical with Frank Wildhorn and is currently writing her second book, entitled "Musical Theatre Training: Lessons from the Broadway Theatre Project."

Related-interest titles from University Press of Florida

Acts of Light: Martha Graham in the Twenty-first Century
Photographs by John Deane, text by Nan Deane Cano

The Art of Teaching Ballet: Ten Twentieth-Century Masters
Gretchen Ward Warren

By With To and From: A Lincoln Kirstein Reader
Edited by Nicholas Jenkins

Caribbean Dance from Abakuá to Zouk: How Movement Shapes Identity
Edited by Susanna Sloat

Classical Ballet Technique
Gretchen Ward Warren

Dance and Music: A Guide to Dance Accompaniment for Musicians and Dance Teachers
Harriet Cavalli

Getting Closer: A Dancer's Perspective
Rosalie O'Connor

Martha Graham: The Evolution of Her Dance Theory and Training, Revised Edition
Marian Horosko

May O'Donnel: Modern Dance Pioneer
Marian Horosko

Pas de Deux: A Textbook on Partnering, Second Edition
Nikolai Serebrennikov

Suki Schorer on Balanchine Technique
Suki Schorer with Russell Lee

Teaching Classical Ballet
John White

Writing in the Dark, Dancing in The New Yorker
Arlene Croce

For more information on these and other books, visit our Web site at www.upf.com.